Help! I'm a
SMALL CHURCH
Youth Worker
Achieving Big-Time Success in a Non-Mega Ministry

D1472639

Help! I'm a
SMALL CHURCH
Youth Worker
Achieving Big-Time Success in a Non-Mega Ministry

RICH GRASSEL

Youth Specialties

ZONDERVAN™

GRAND RAPIDS, MICHIGAN 49530

www.zondervan.com

Help! I'm a Small Church Youth Worker! Achieving Big-Time Success in a Non-Mega Ministry

Copyright © 2002 by Youth Specialties

Youth Specialties Books, 300 S. Pierce St., El Cajon, CA 92020, are published by Zondervan, 5300 Patterson Ave. S.E., Grand Rapids, MI 49530.

Library of Congress Cataloging-in-Publication Data

Grassel, Rich. 1960—
   Help! I'm a Small Church Youth Worker : achieving big-time success in a non-mega ministry / Rich Grassel.
      p. cm.
   ISBN 0-310-23946-X
 1. Church work with youth. 2. Small churches. I. Title
   BV4447 .G665 2002
   259' .23—dc21

                                 2002005472

Web site addresses listed in this book were current at the time of publication. Please contact Youth Specialties via e-mail (YS@YouthSpecialties.com) to report URLs that are no longer operational and replacement URLs if available.

Edited by Sally Corran and Dave Urbanski
Cover and interior design by Unidea

Printed in the United States of America

01 02 03 04 05 06 07 / / 10 9 8 7 6 5 4 3 2 1

Dedication and Acknowledgments

Thank you...

Dean Smith (department chair, Bible) and my immediate supervisor, Brad Frey—*for the encouragement and support.*

Kovonne Compaan—*for being a great reader.*

Dick Riedel—*a committed pastor, supportive mentor, and treasured friend.*

Our First Presbyterian Church family in Lancaster, Ohio—*for your boundless love, kindness, and many precious friendships.*

The community of Lancaster (our first true community home) and two of their finest ministers, Steve Schellin and Jeff Connar—*you all gave an undeserving young man ("small" in ability and ministry experience) a gracious opportunity to become a little more that what he was before he came there. Collectively we worked hard to pursue our vision of student ministry and learned how to touch, not only the future, but eternity as well. May the Lord richly bless you for your love, character, concern, and selfless investment in the lives of students.* "The net result of all Student Ministry is to create Servant Leaders who will change the world for Christ."

My family—*my wife, Ruth, and sons, Jeremiah and Jordan, for sharing me with so many others so that I could do this project.*

"And I searched for a man among them who should build up the wall and stand in the gap, before Me for the land, that I should not destroy it; but I found no one."

Ezekiel 22:30 (NASB)

CONTENTS

Models That'll Fit to a "T":
Four Approaches to Youth Ministry in the Small Church

"Who You Callin' Small?"

When I was still writing this book, a local youth minister of a large church asked me about the subject of my research. I proudly replied, "Youth ministry in the small church." He suppressed a wince, but still managed to ask, "Why are you writing on youth ministry in the *small* church?" (He might as well have asked, "Why not something more worthwhile?")

My answer then—and now—is very simple: Because youth ministry in the small church, believe it or not, is the most prevalent kind of youth ministry in America.

The small church

Typically, a small church contains fewer than 150 participants. These churches comprise between **85 and 90 percent** of churches in our country (about 300,000 churches out of 340,000). That's right. That means there's probably a better than eight in 10 chance that *you,* the reader of these words, are a small church youth worker. (Which also means that probably better than 80 percent of youth workers should *buy* this book! But I digress…)

When I use the term "large church," I refer to churches with 600 or more regular participants—this includes megachurches. In other words, the remaining 10 to 15 percent of American churches. (But remember this, too: Churches with as many as 250 participants might share the same characteristics as much smaller churches!) George Barna, in *Boiling Point*, reports that only two to three percent of these churches have 1,000 members or more. Most find this stat unbelievable—because it defys the perception that large churches are plentiful.

Misperceptions of small churches

Contrary to common perceptions, small churches are **not dying**; in fact, they continue to emerge, not only in America, but also worldwide. Among the many reasons why folks like you choose to minister in small church settings is because they offer something that many large churches can't—community. (We'll cover that a little later.)

Another common misperception of the small church is that it's ineffective. Why? Because it's not a large church. "Huh?" you ask. It's pretty simple, actually: *Since so many judge success by numbers, the small church is usually (and immediately) discounted as ineffective.*

Another is that the small church is spiritually dead (i.e., if it isn't growing, it must be dying). On the contrary, the small church can often nurture its members more effectively than the megachurch down the block.

And on and on and on…

Accurate perceptions of small churches

In his book, *Entering the World of the Small Church*, Anthony Pappas offers *balanced* insights on the nature of most small churches. Some of his characteristics are encouraging; some aren't. I list both here—because if you intend to do youth ministry in a small church (and survive), you need to know the good, the bad, and the ugly.

According to Pappas—
• The small church is a stable, not dynamic, organization.
• It's a "little world unto itself."
• It sees the past but not the future.
• It functions out of habit, not strategic planning.

- It functions like a family (enmeshed and intimate) as opposed to an organization (structured and businesslike).
- It's based on personal relationships.
- It's based on experience, not theory.

Pretty different from the large church, which is most often characterized as dynamic, outgoing, professional, and focused on budgeting and planning.

Bigger isn't always better!

If you've read this far, you obviously need help. (Er, umm…certainly not in the "get your head examined" sense, but rather in the…oh, never mind!) You're probably interested in or are already doing youth ministry in a small church.

Well, you're in luck. *Help! I'm a Small Church Youth Worker!* does just that.

On nearly all relevant quality factors, larger churches compare unfavorably with smaller ones. Here are just two examples. In the minichurches (under 100) 31 percent of all in attendance have, according to the pastor, an assignment corresponding to their gifts; in megachurches, this figure is a mere 17 percent. In minichurches, 46 percent of those who attend services have been integrated into a small group, whereas in megachurches this is true of only 12 percent. The scenario is just as dramatic for nearly all of the 170 variables that we used to rate a church's quality.
—Christian A. Schwarz,
Natural Church Development
(The largest ever study of its kind—two million participants)

This little book fills a huge void. For example, have you noticed that many of the youth ministry books on the market are written for youth workers in large churches? That the ideas, games, and activities in them are geared toward youth ministries in large churches? Have you noticed that most youth ministry training is geared toward large-church youth workers? And in the meantime almost 90 percent of the churches out there are ignored.

In response, what I've tried to do in *Help! I'm a Small Church Youth Worker!* is highlight the characteristics that make small churches different than large churches. And I note that because small churches are different, their youth ministry programs, in turn, have different needs. So, it's important that you see your ministry development as a process of *understanding*; first knowing your Ministry Context, then choosing

> *Just 'cause you ain't runnin' with the big dogs don't mean you oughta be a copycat. (Mixed metaphor...I know, I know.)*
> *Give yourself permission to do things differently!*

your Ministry Methods, and finally growing into your own Ministry Model.

In the first section, Out of Context, Outta Luck, I offer guidelines for determining what resources small churches should offer their kids—in light of probable limitations—as well as ministry methods. In the second section, Models That'll Fit You to a "T," I provide ideas for different ways to approach developing programs based on your church's ministry context.

That's about the size of it. (Pun intended!)

Whatever you glean from this book, remember this: *Bigger isn't always better!*

OUT OF CONTEXT, OUTTA LUCK

The Importance of Ministry Context, Ministry Methods, and the Unique Characteristics of the Small Church

1
The Dreaded
Question

It was the end of the day—and the end of a week of inspiring youth ministry seminars. We were a cheerful group of about a dozen youth workers, comfortably seated around the dinner table, all of differing ages, regions, denominations…and church sizes.

Our conversation began innocently enough, sparked by what we'd heard from seminar leaders earlier in the day. But then one of the large church youth workers asked *the dreaded question*:

"So…how big is your youth ministry?"

The large church youth workers responded immediately and with great enthusiasm, listing their expansive, active memberships, noting their state-of-the-art ministry resources, and sharing their awesome visions and strategies for additional growth. Feeling woefully inadequate, we small church youth workers grew increasingly quiet. Our confidence and cheerfulness evaporated.

Later in the evening, a few of us vented in the hotel lounge (actually we were completely exasperated!). After some reflection, we noted a number of ways that our churches differed from large churches—mainly in areas related to environment, expectations, and goals. And it became clear to our group: *We need something different, because we **are** different!* Not incompetent—just different.

In other words, small church youth workers need a specialized approach to youth ministry.

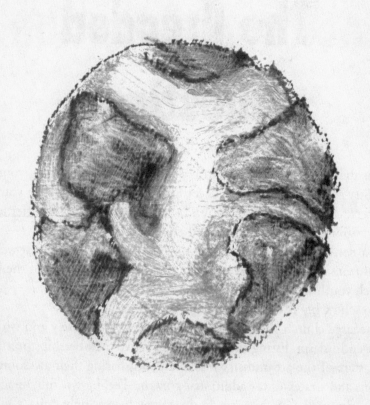

2
Location, Location, Location

Why are there so many small churches?

It's important to keep in mind that a huge percentage of small churches couldn't be anything but small. Why? Because there aren't enough people living around them! In vast stretches of our country, there simply isn't the population density for large churches—or the numbers to allow for huge youth ministry programs.

> The midwestern city of Columbus, Ohio, has almost 660,000 residents; *the entire state of Wyoming* has fewer than 500,000 residents.

Why does church location affect my ministry?

There are small churches everywhere, from the big city to the farmland. Their geographies directly affect their special cultures and needs—their particular personalities, values, and traditions. So...everything from cultural and ethnic issues to transportation and travel can (and will) have an enormous impact on how youth workers in small churches develop their programs.

But before you begin ministry at your small church, you should be aware of some location-specific issues for churches in urban, inner-ring, suburban, small-town, and rural locations.

Urban Locations

Youth workers in small, urban churches face a number of issues that other small churches don't face. Be prepared for the following:

1. **Limited finances**—even less cash than the average small church.
2. **Safety**—crime and dangerous areas might affect meeting times, locations, and frequency.
3. **Multi-ethnicity**—not just African Americans and Latinos, but also Europeans, Southeast Asians, Russians…in short, *every* nationality!
4. **Acute family problems**—young single mothers, absentee fathers, and often grandparents and other family members as guardians.
5. **Limited mobility**—public transportation might be students' only way to youth group activities.
6. **Significant poverty**—many single mothers struggle to provide, and fathers might be out of work.
7. **Poor health**—often families can't afford medical assistance.
8. **Violence**—for inner-city kids, it's a daily concern, and they may be afraid to attend youth group events because of it. (Between 7 and 9 p.m. in the summer can be the most dangerous time to hold youth group meetings in the inner-city.)
9. **Fear of teenagers**—older people in the community might suspect their young neighbors are "always up to no good."
10. **Dilapidated buildings, limited space and out-of-date facilities**—the church sanctuary might be the only decent meeting room available to you.
11. **High student turnover**—youth group kids may not stick around because of their parents' employment situations or other family problems.

If you plan to do youth ministry in a small, urban church, these sorts of issues must factor into the way you structure your programs. Kids in inner-city churches are aware of these issues, and if they and the congregation realize you're aware, too, you'll eliminate at least one hurdle.

> In urban churches, you might have to deal with gang-related issues. If you don't have experience dealing with gangs, don't attempt it without help from very experienced people. (And even if you do have expertise—seek help anyway!) There are ministries established specifically to deal with gang members.

Inner-Ring Locations

The "inner ring" is positioned between suburban and urban areas and is often made up of older neighborhoods. The churches here are usually older, too. Often these churches grow slowly and don't attract new families. It's not uncommon for them to have a mix of blue- and white-collar workers. Generally, youth workers in small, inner-ring churches will face these issues:

> Try starting youth group meetings at 7 or 7:30 on weeknights to avoid traffic tie-ups. Consider an after-school program if you live near a school.

1. **Competition from larger churches with aggressive outreach programs**—in small areas, the word about good programs gets around pretty quick!
2. **Transportation problems**—rush-hour traffic and bad weather can dissuade students who have to travel more than 20 minutes to youth group events.

> Obtain athletic and activity schedules from school districts represented in your youth group. Plan all activities well in advance, balancing them between school calendars, your church's schedule, and ministry opportunities.

> Plan fundraisers and inexpensive retreats and events. Doing this will increase participation and therefore build community. Make this a part of your youth ministry programming—don't view it as an add-on.

3. **School and neighborhood loyalty**—kids from rival schools and areas may not want to hang out with your kids (this can apply to adults, too!).
4. **Financial difficulties**—inner-ring families on fixed incomes usually don't have a lot of discretionary cash.
5. **Denominational loyalty**—adults in various congregations, particulary those in leadership, are often dedicated to carrying on their families' denominational traditions…and are suspicious of others.

Suburban Locations

Of all the small churches, suburban congregations tend to have the easiest access to materials and leadership. In addition, the members of these churches are typically young, white-collar workers who are educated and business-minded. Youth workers in small suburban churches should be prepared for the following issues:

1. **Turnover in student population**—parents often move because of transfers and promotions.
2. **Education**—parents expect their kids to go to college, and most kids expect the same.
3. **Mobility of students**—they or their friends typically own cars.
4. **Social sophistication**—students are concerned about their social status and are introduced to social events early.
5. **Overbooked schedules**—involvement in sports, clubs, and other activities leaves little time for youth group.

> Tweny minutes is the magic time limit! Although your sophomores, juniors, and seniors might be able to drive to events—even ones more than 20 minutes away—parents must drive your junior highers and freshmen. And if parents have to drive more than 20 minutes, often they won't—and those kids will stay home.

Because kids in suburbia are so busy, Sunday night is often the only night they have available to devote to youth group.

6. **Potentially less support from parents**—because of their own schedules, youth group might be low on parents' priority lists.
7. **Conflicting schedules**—many different schools, public and private, might be represented in your youth ministry and their schedules often conflict.
8. **Expansion**—many small suburban congregations want to grow.
9. **High expectations**—they have higher budgets to pay youth workers…and they expect their money's worth.
10. **Often more corporate**—though still family-oriented.
11. **Cash flow**—often families with money to spend will move on quickly.

Small-Town Locations

Statistics show that two-thirds of all small chuches come from small towns of 10,000 or less—that's 200,000 churches! There are, perhaps, more small churches in small towns than anywhere else in the country. Depending on the industry and history of the small town, the types of people in these congregations can vary widely. Similarly, there is no one dominant denomination in these churches. There are, however, some issues all small town youth workers should know about:
1. **Loose denominational commitments**—neighbors and friends may attend different churches, so they feel comfortable crossing church borders.
2. **Lack of community growth**—but the metropolitan and suburban areas are expanding.

Because they don't have the policy restrictions of larger, city schools, small town schools might be willing to work with the church to establish youth programs.

Work in harmony with (and often deference to) schools and other community programs; you might get to see your students more often this way.

3. **More church-member involvement in youth group**—for better or worse, more people in the church feel responsible for the kids.
4. **More time**—students' schedules might not be super-packed, so they have more free time for church...*or for not-so-good activities.*

> Rural youth workers should not be surprised if they encounter problems similar to those that plague urban and suburban kids. In January 2000, a study entitled "No Place to Hide" was presented at a mayors' conference. This study listed the following statistics for rural eighth graders in comparison with urban eighth graders:
>
> It's more than twice as likely that rural eighth graders have smoked cigarettes and nearly five times as likely that they've used smokeless tobacco compared to rural eighth graders.
>
> It's 29 percent more likely that they've used alcohol.
>
> It's 70 percent more likely that they've been intoxicated.
>
> It's 34 percent more likely that they've smoked marijuana.
>
> It's twice as likely that they've used amphetamines.
>
> It's 83 percent more likely that they've used crack cocaine.

Rural Locations

Unfortunately, when most people think of small churches, they picture tiny, dying churches in Podunkville. But don't be surprised if thousands of rural churches in America start growing. Eric Pooley, in an article titled "The Great Escape" (*Time,* Dec. 8, 1997), reports that in the last decade, "rural America has enjoyed a net inflow of 2 million Americans.... Thanks to the newcomers, 75 percent of the nation's rural counties are growing again after years of decline." Keeping this in mind, the rural youth worker should be aware of the following issues:

1. **Tiny numbers**—there aren't many families to draw from (yet).
2. **Paid youth workers? Ha!**—sometimes small rural churches can't even afford part-time youth workers for the few kids in attendance (or full-time pastors!).

> **Don't fight the County Fair! Incorporate it into your program.**

> Rural people tend to appreciate hard, physical labor. When visiting your rural students, consider offering to help bale hay, feed the animals, and water the garden. Your crediblity is at stake here!

3. **Limited resources**—buildings might be old, and money is mostly scarce.
4. **Limited education**—many adults have attained a high school education (or less), and many of the students may not get much further. So be careful how you talk—avoid sophisticated airs with some.
5. **Travel problems**—distances between friends, schools, and church can be huge, and bad weather will add to the difficulty of these long trips.
6. **Low participation**—parents of rural kids are more likely to require their teenagers to help with the business or the house before they can go to youth group.
7. **Seasonal events**—harvest time, county fairs, local parades and events are highly important.

> Keep the seasons in mind (and the special communal and individual needs associated with them): Field work is done in the summer; harvest and county fairs are in the fall; travel is "iffy" in the winter; and planting is done in the spring.

8. **Schools and community involvement**—schools and communities, for better or worse, may desire involvement in church youth programs.
9. **Cultural preservation**—rural folk expect their youth workers to value the rural lifestyle.

3
Faith Traditions Do Matter!

Why must small churches be so loyal to their denominations?

Often small churches look to their denominational leaders to give them guidance during pastoral changes, when there's conflict in the congregation, and, of course, during financial crises. Their denominational affiliation is often their strongest base of support. (Note: A *denomination* and a *faith tradition* is not always the same. Plus, many small churches don't belong to particular denominations, but do belong to particular practices of faith traditions.)

Being denominationally bound can strengthen a church in some areas and weaken it in others. The strengths can develop from shared resources, the weaknesses from denominational policies. Although some members, particularly teenagers, may not feel tied to denominational policies, the church as a whole may feel constrained by them. In many cases, the churches are not confident enough to determine their own policies. One small church leader summarized these feelings succinctly: "Those are the rules!"

I worked in one church that wanted as many of its youth as possible to attend a national conference the denomination was hosting. But the expenses for transportation, conference registration, and food were too high for most of the families to afford. Nevertheless, the church wouldn't permit our youth group to plan fundraisers to help with the costs. Why? Denominational traditions wouldn't allow it—those were the rules.

> **"When you marry a person, you marry her family"; when you work in a small church, you work within its denomination—and that means adhering to its policies.**

Potential theological hazards

Not long ago, a youth worker told me he had been fired even though his program was growing, his students loved him, he was organized, and his leadership team was strong. It turns out he was fired because neither he nor his students could articulate their brand of faith *well enough* to suit the church. It's not that he wasn't being biblical—he certainly was. It's just that he wasn't teaching the letter of denominational doctrine.

This situation is not uncommon. Many youth workers are at churches from denominations different from their own experiences and education. Of course, that combination can surface all kinds of problems. Unfortunately, it's the kids who get caught in the middle. Despite this danger, many small churches still recruit and hire youth leaders with no training in their particular theological traditions—and youth workers ignorant of their churches' theology risk losing their positions and disrupting their churches. *Understanding church/denominational doctrine and creeds is absolutely essential.*

> **Sadly, some small churches with limited means repeatedly turn away from other youth ministry resources outside their denominations or traditions. They even openly discourage kids from participating in anything not associated with their home church. These attitudes prevail even as their young men and women leave their congregation because the church leaders are more concerned about tradition than youth's spiritual growth.**

Because of this, youth workers should ask and answer the following questions before accepting a position and planning a youth program:

1. *What are the creeds and doctrines of this denomination?*
2. *Do I agree with them, and can I teach and model them in my life?*
3. *Can I represent them with integrity?*
4. *How does the church administration feel about the denominational policies?*
5. *How does the congregation feel about them?*
6. *How will the denomination's and church's traditions and doctrines impact my approach to youth ministry?*
7. *What strategies and methods should I adopt because of those traditions?*

What spiritual growth and maturity looks like in different theological traditions

In developing an approach to ministering to their students, small church youth workers might find it helpful to identify the differences between some of the major church denominations as they pertain to spiritual maturity. Most denominations are connected to historical traditions: reformed, evangelical, holiness or Wesleyan, charismatic or Pentecostal, Anglican, Catholic, orthodox, liturgical. **Clearly, the forthcoming descriptions won't be representative of all churches from all traditions, but they do offer general ideas regarding the more fundamental beliefs of each.** Different faith traditions and denominations have different ideas regarding what spiritual maturity looks like in students as well.

Be aware that kids in all traditions can talk the church's talk and walk the church's walk, yet still have no idea what it means to know that Christ *lives in them*.

The Reformed Tradition

Most reformed traditions are based on the Westminster and Augsburg Confessions of Faith. They supplement these with other doctrines and creeds supported by Scripture. Youth workers in reformed churches must know Reformed Theology. In addition, they must know how to teach it in a manner that makes it a vital part of their students' spiritual lives.

> The word "theology" came from the Greek word "theologia," which meant: "to study the knowledge of God in such a way that it became a part of you."
>
> **—Anglican theologian J.I. Packer**

Here are some main thrusts of reformed churches:

- An intellectual approach to faith.
- Many want to have committees or church leaders approve your study materials before you use them.
- Some emphasize having parents work with their own children as a part of the youth ministry program.
- Most want the congregation involved in decisions about the program.
- Many welcome having kids involved in other areas of the church.
- They expect students to be "theologically articulate" and involved in Bible study. If students meet these expectations, they'll be regarded as spiritually mature.

The Evangelical Tradition

This tradition emphasizes biblical knowledge. Many independent, community, and small denominations come from this tradition. Although Scripture memorization is important, broad theological principles rather than specific doctrines take precedence. It's important that students in this tradition understand how Scripture and these theological principles apply to their lives. This is huge!

If you're a youth worker in this tradition, you should emphasize biblical knowledge, and at the same time teach how the church sees

Scripture manifested in the lives of its members. Again, you should remember that just because kids know verses and principles doesn't mean that they have internalized this knowledge into a vibrant faith.

Here are some important aspects of the evangelical tradition:

- The congregation expects all teaching to include Scripture references.
- It believes all members (adults and youth) should be involved in Bible studies.
- Parents expect their kids to be self-motivated in their personal spiritual growth.
- Members, especially kids, can compartmentalize their lives, leaving God at church and their actions at school.
- They expect discipleship and outreach to the community.
- Students are often considered spiritually mature if they can pinpoint their salvation experience, have regular devotions, and know Scripture.

The Holiness or Wesleyan Tradition

Churches in the holiness or Wesleyan tradition look for "holiness" and "godliness" as evidence of Christian maturity. This often means they expect their members to be modestly dressed, abstain from alcohol, and avoid movies, music, dancing, and certain books and magazines. It's not uncommon for those who work in these churches to be required to sign contracts stating that they won't participate in any activity the denomination frowns upon. Unfortunately, many of these youth workers—even those who're aware of these requirements—have lost their positions because of their failure to uphold them.

In many cases, churches in the holiness or Wesleyan tradition view the world as fallen and depraved, so good Christians should avoid contact with it as much as possible. In some instances, parents and church leaders will want to know that their students have had a "crisis experience." This is when one feels a sudden change brought on by the Holy Spirit so that they virtually no longer desire anything "sinful."

Here's what to look for in churches from the Holiness or Wesleyan tradition:

- Many expect their ministers to be able to teach and model the church's concept of "holy" living.
- Many don't allow leaders to use pop culture, not even as a teaching device.
- Often the types of camps and conferences their kids can attend are denominationally bound.
- All teaching must use Scripture directly.
- Many emphasize a literal interpretation of the Bible.
- Students are considered spiritually mature if they've had a crisis experience and live holy, non-worldly lives.

The Charismatic or Pentecostal Tradition

Typically, churches in the charismatic or Pentecostal tradition are concerned with the gifts of the Holy Spirit. In addition, emphasis is placed on the power of the Holy Spirit to change their lives dramatically. They believe Christians should have very personal and intimate relationships with God, Jesus, and the Holy Spirit. The language these congregations uses reflects this intimacy.

Youth workers, then, will be expected to use and teach this kind of language and produce experiences that will enable students to use their spiritual gifts. Being able to exhibit these gifts is regarded as a "blessing of the Holy Spirit." According to the tradition, failure to do so might indicate "unresolved personal sin" or lack of faith.

Here are some important aspects of churches in the charismatic or Pentecostal tradition:

- They value music, audiovisual technology, and emotionally powerful teaching.
- They encourage spontaneous reaction to the Holy Spirit.
- Some develop a spiritual hierarchy based on spiritual gifts.
- Many expect struggles to disappear when kids are "touched by the Spirit."
- Most expect their youth to be involved in all aspects of the church.

- Students are considered spiritually mature if they demonstrate evidence of spiritual gifts and a radical willingness to follow Christ.

The Liturgical or High Church Tradition

In churches with highly liturgical traditions (such as Episcopalian, Roman Catholic, and Eastern Orthodox), maintaining reverence for the customs of the church is tantamount. In some of these liturgical churches, Protestant and Reformed theology is also important. Primarily, though, all church members are expected to participate in the sacraments and understand the creeds of the church.

Youth workers in these churches will be expected to teach these traditions. Students should participate in the liturgy and understand the meaning and history behind it. Failure to emphasize these customs can be seen as a failure to uphold the church's values.

Here are some aspects of highly liturgical churches:

- They expect full family participation in all areas of the church.
- They value the practice of the sacraments and church doctrine, creeds, and customs of the early church fathers.
- Some want creeds and doctrines used in addition to Scripture as the model for the Christian life.
- Many are concerned with social justice issues.
- Church tradition is often equal in authority to the Bible.
- Students are considered spiritually mature if they practice and value the sacraments, creeds, and liturgy, as well as respect church tradition.

4

It's a Family Affair (Not a Corporate Entity)

Why do people like small churches?

In short, simplicity, intimacy, connectedness, and familial feelings. Also, membership is often important because small church members see it as a commitment to the church "family." These are legitimate desires and preferences and ought to be appreciated and respected by the entire church.

But these attributes also can make it difficult to do youth ministry. Why? **Because ministry principles are based on a family structure rather than on a corporate structure.** Rather than functioning as a business where each employee is hired to perform a task, the small church functions as an extended family.

In fact, it is!

In many small churches, leaders come from only a few families who control much of what happens at the church. Youth workers in small churches must learn to work with these families and within the church family structure.

Selling out is not an option in youth ministry. But it's advisable to understand the political landscape and respect how it works.

Family politics

In many small churches, power and influence is normally shared between the pastor and about three to five families. It's important to understand this dynamic if it exists in your church. Youth workers who fail here often fail in their jobs. This doesn't mean they should suck up; it just means they should be sensitive to these issues.

Here are some helpful tips for working with those powerful families in the small church:

- Find out where the power centers are *without playing the politics.*
- Take time to learn the pet projects and values of these families; they will appreciate this.
- Be prepared for disagreement between families; your words and ideas can be misused, too, so guard your tongue.
- Be aware that your students also know who gets along and who doesn't.
- Treat all students the same, even if students from certain families expect special attention.

Youth workers in small churches must recognize that certain families just won't get along. Whether the bad blood began because of theological differences, power struggles, or failed personal relationships, these families still hold a grudge. They even may have forgotten what conflict was! This can make it difficult to minister to students from these families. Youth workers may have to play the part of reconciler before they can begin to create a youth group.

In many small churches, particularly in small towns and rural areas, much of the congregation will be linked by blood or marriage to three to five families—that could be as much as 75 to 80 percent of the total population of the church. Mismanage or insult one member of the family, and you have insulted them all.

Why don't many small churches have separate programs for youth?

It's not uncommon to have several families in a small church that believe youth ministry should not be farmed out to youth workers. In many cases, pastors and their congregations believe it's solely the family's responsibility to minister to the kids in the church. This philosophy is taken from Malachi 4:6: "He will turn the hearts of the fathers to their children, and the hearts of the children to their fathers." Youth ministry, then, is a family enterprise with communal support from the congregation. It's also not uncommon that congregations are divided over this issue.

Because of this perspective, youth workers won't be able to do much of their work without the permission from (or involvement with) the entire congregation. These folks want to be a part of the decision-making process...although they, unfortunately, may not support it with their time and energy.

In some cases, all generations of the church are involved in all aspects of the church. This **intergenerational culture** has benefits as well as obstacles. Here are some things to expect:

- Adults may spontaneously join in some of your youth programs. They may feel more ownership, personal responsibility, and comfort with certain kids because of past, close associations with them. This can make discussions about certain topics and relationships with certain kids awkward, but the bonds that form can help the kids, too.

- There might be a less intense, less pronounced "youth culture," because the boundaries between adults and kids fade more gradually into each other.

- More adults will feel free to make comments and suggestions about how to run the youth programs. Don't take this personally—and make sure your responses aren't offensive (or come across as defensive).

- Students may not be able to participate in certain functions because of their commitments to other areas of the church.

A Family Decision

A number of years ago, one of my youth ministry students was interviewing for an internship as a part-time youth minister in a local small church. He interviewed with me and the pastor, the search committee, and church elders. The vote was unanimous. Everyone was excited . . . until one of the elders asked, "When does the congregation get to vote?" The pastor responded by stating that it wasn't necessary for the congregation to vote, because they voted for the session (governing body of the church), and the session represents the congregation. The elder grew red in the face and sputtered angrily, "I will not stand by and permit the rest of the session and pastor to *ramrod* this decision down the rest of the church's throat!" There was a long pause, and then someone suggested that the young man be presented to the congregation for a vote. Pacified, the elder relaxed, and they went on with other business.

The issue wasn't just a church elder who was being difficult. It was an elder who felt that a new *family member* couldn't be invited into the church unless the rest of the family agreed. This was a family matter, and all of the family should be in on it.

> There is no anonymity in a small church; your business is everyone else's business.

Why don't small churches grow?

For the small church, it's all about *relationships*—taking care of the people who you know best. **Success and failure in your ministry will be determined more by the quality of your relationships with church members, rather than how many students you have coming to your program.** Small churches don't necessarily expect huge numbers, but they do expect positive relationships with their kids and with the adults as well. Standoffishness or isolation is asking for a quick ticket to the door.

Here are some ideas for working within family structure of small churches:

- Take care of the students in your church first. Build relationships and let them be the recipients of your best efforts before you do anything outside the church.
- Spend time learning how people are connected to each other and what their issues and commitments to one another may be.

> Early in the summer, we had our annual Sunday school picnic at a beautiful park. I had invited a number of neighborhood middle-school teenagers. While not strangers to the church, they were not members, either. Many of these teens—the males—were first in line, wolfed down their food, and got right back in line. I didn't know about their second trip until I heard the sharp crack of a spatula coming down on the hand of one the older teenagers. A matriarch of one of the church families squawked, "You've had enough food! My grandson hasn't had his food yet! Now get out of line." Moving toward the commotion, I asked what the problem was. Her response was definitive: "They aren't even members of our church!"

- Reach new kids in the community through church kids. Church members will interpret this as helping their families and neighbors as well. Inviting students who have no connection to the church invites suspicion and resentment, especially if resources, scholarships, and (yes) food are involved.
- Make sure outreach is part of your job description and be ready with Scripture to support it as a missions ministry.
- Take volunteers not connected to the church through proper relational channels so the rest of the church can become comfortable with them.

> One of my small churches raised money and collected food every Thanksgiving and Christmas. At the right time it was given away, but always first to the "needy" families within the church. A few people in the community became recipients, but only after church families were served.

Why don't small churches try new things?

Because the majority of small church members hail from blue-collar and service-oriented occupations, their experiences tend to prevent them from seeing and living life in a broad, "possibilities-oriented" fashion. Motivation to make changes in the church's ministries is rarely influenced by hope for the future, but rather what has been tried and true. And if you do get around to implementing new ideas, the results had better be immediate!

If you use terms such as *development* or *investment* when describing your ministry to these small church members, be prepared for possible animosity. These are white-collar business terms from corporate America—the enemy of many blue-collar small towns! Similarly, many members are put off by youthful energy and change. This applies to the senior pastor, too, who might be threatened by a youth worker's newfangled plans.

It'd be nice if there were sure methods for dealing with these issues, but there aren't. In many small churches, these issues are a fact of life.

But never fear! There are tips available. Here are a few:

- Learn to work through the pastor and influential members of the church to get new and innovative projects off the ground.
- Learn to motivate leaders within the here-and-now framework of time. Teach and demonstrate what adults can do "today" or "this week" that will make a difference in kids' lives.

> The second leading cause of youth worker turnover every 18 to 24 months is the inability to manage a successful youth ministry in light of a senior pastor's fragile ego. It's not unlike the biblical story in which the people sang, "Saul has killed his thousands... David his ten thousands..."

- Make sure all your proposals and ideas travel through channels of authority. People expect to be informed, especially those serving on committees; they hate surprises!

- Share your vision for the youth group through regular newsletters, committee reports, and annual meetings.
- Use language church members will understand. Avoid pop culture terminology if they won't like or understand it.
- Learn to minister to your pastor: leave encouraging notes; invite him to lunch; affirm her publicly; defer and refer to his leadership.
- Don't participate in students' or parents' complaint sessions regarding your pastor; instead, emphasize things he does well.
- Share the wealth of your success with other volunteers and leaders.

Some churches are small because they split from or are a satellite branch from a large church. Usually these churches value outreach, evangelism, and growth. Typically, these churches are more open to creative and alternative ministry.

5

Diversity and Divisiveness

Why is it sometimes so difficult for some small church youth groups to establish a sense of community?

Years ago I walked into the junior and senior high Sunday school room at a small church. I was the new youth pastor, and it was my job to resurrect what has once been a vital program. As I surveyed the room, I marveled that there was absolutely no conversation. The "alternative" kids sat passively on old, worn-out living room furniture. The token jock and prep were stretched out, pretending (I hoped) to be asleep. Only a few of these kids went to the same school together.

As the year progressed, little changed. There was no community. There were even adversarial relationships. Although there were other problems in the church that contributed to this divisiveness, clearly the dominant problem was "subcultural diversity." Until I dealt with that, nothing I did to develop a strong youth program would be effective.

When it comes to developing a sense of community, many small churches struggle with a kind of subcultural diversity. The more diverse the youth group, the more difficult it is to establish community. First, students don't share the history of their parents (who've known each other forever). Second, suburban small churches tend to represent multiple school systems more than any other church, and this creates an enormous community dynamic. Third, students from different socioeconomic backgrounds sometimes don't mix well.

> Although *The Breakfast Club* has a great philosophy behind it—all high school kids have similar needs and problems—it's still a movie. Don't expect the same type of interaction between subcultures in your youth group. After all, even the kids in the movie realized they wouldn't talk with each other again once they were around their other friends.

Why should youth workers cater to teenage subcultures?

Kids belong to their cliques for a number of reasons, some petty, others painful. But most kids feel a deep attachment to their subculture and are proud of their differences. Any attempts to reach those kids will succeed only if you realize and respect those differences.

Many subcultures are developed due to kids' shared interests or other commonalities: Ethnic backgrounds, music and fashion, extracurricular activities, family problems, and shared experiences. But in the small church, some of the most common are those based on economic standing, social status, life stages, and geography.

Here are some problems that arise from each one, and some tips for dealing with them:

> In some unfortunate instances, one subculture will tend toward dominance and drive away almost all the kids from other subcultures—a kind of Social Darwinism.

Economic Standing

Sharon sat quietly on the bus, despite the loud chatter from her fellow junior highers. She was excited about the ski trip with her youth group, but she was nervous as well. This really was her last attempt at "fitting in," she told herself. Her parents weren't sophisticated like the other kids' parents. Besides, she couldn't keep up. The other girls her age had beautiful clothes, the most fashionable haircuts, their own ski equipment, and money to buy whatever snacks, food, and souvenirs they wanted. Sharon's spending money was a combination of prize money from entering her goats in the county fair and a little extra her mother was able to scrape from the family budget. This difference was obvious to the other girls as well, and they let her know it. She would see how it would go over the weekend, but this time, the others would have to show some initiative. If it didn't get any better, this would be the last time she would come to any youth group activity. (And it was.)

Students live in a highly competitive world. One of the fiercest areas of competition is family wealth. It's not uncommon for many students to flaunt their material fortune. Similarly, it's not uncommon for students from a family of limited means to be intimidated by or even resentful of those with more.

In small churches, the differences are much more visible, so these tensions are heightened. This problem also can keep youth workers from being able to develop a strong sense of community.

Many small church youth groups have difficulty coming together when both blue- and white-collar families are represented. In order to begin building a community, you must recognize that economic difference is a problem. Then, you have to deal with it.

Here are some tips:

- Treat all students the same; the wealthy kids will notice if you favor those with less money…and vice versa.
- Plan activities that all students can afford.
- Have fundraisers and develop scholarships so those who can't afford certain activities can still participate.

- Communicate in a clear, gracious, but firm manner that economic discrimination won't be tolerated.

Social Status

"I'm cold!" one of my popular girls complained. This was the day our middle-school kids were participating in a workday at a local camp. "Here," replied one of my not-so-popular guys, "use my sweatshirt." Fearing her peers would mock her, she responded, "No thanks!" and threw the non-name brand sweatshirt back, hitting the guy in the face.

We all wish this were not a problem, but the reality is that certain students see themselves in a higher social class than others. Anyone who has done youth ministry for even a short period can tell both horror (and hilarious) stories of the wild machinations kids will go through to avoid sitting next to the wrong person or to squeeze in next to the right one. Unfortunately, even in the funny stories, rejected kids feel very acute pain.

In small churches, these social status rifts can be even more pronounced. Group chemistry, therefore, can be very difficult to achieve. Many students who enjoy significant social status are terrified to associate with students of lesser social status because word will get around quickly in a small church. On the flip side, unpopular kids are often intimidated by the popular ones and are reluctant to initiate relationships.

There are some ways of dealing with this, though:

- Address this discrimination as early as you can. Begin building relationships and breaking down barriers as soon as kids enter the youth group.
- Never tolerate "exclusive" behavior. Always attack it quickly, firmly, and sensitively. Remember, the students who are socially exclusive were taught those values, most likely by their parents.
- Be aware of your body language and speech. Kids pick up those signals instantly, and they will notice any differences in your physical reactions.

- Continue to discuss social status issues throughout the year. Having kids share their experiences can help further break down social barriers.
- Employ community-building activities like a ropes course.

Life Stages

One problem in many small churches is that in order to have more than one or two kids at a meeting, different ages and grades have to be combined. A 12-year-old sixth grader might be attending the same meeting as an 18-year-old high school senior. For obvious reasons,

> **While the senior might be concerned about leaving for college, the sixth grader might be concerned about not being chosen to play kickball.**

these students will have a hard time relating to each other.

Usually the junior high kids enjoy combined meetings with senior high kids. But senior highers normally hate it: "What do we have in common with the geeky seventh-graders?" It's hard not to sympathize with senior highers because they realize that at their "life-stage," they have completely different concerns, needs, and levels of maturity. Therefore, in regularly combined youth groups, the senior highers begin to disappear. Although the junior high kids might like being around the older kids, they can be intimidated by them, and encouraging the younger kids to participate can be difficult also.

Although having separate meetings for different grade groupings would be ideal, there are times when groups have to be combined, especially in very small churches. But there are ways of dealing with it:

- Develop senior high leaders who can help run different parts of the meeting (music, games, Bible study, et cetera). This gives them a sense of ownership and leadership.
- Train the older, more mature students as mentors or discipleship partners for the younger ones. Junior high kids will have someone to look up to, and the older kids will see that the younger kids need their guidance.

- Have a separate small-group meeting for the senior highers (even if there are only two). This gives them a chance to interact with you in ways they can't with junior highers around.

Geography

It's amazing how emotional ties to schools and communities can keep students from developing relationships with one another. Students from the same schools and areas of town identify with each other, even if they don't spend that much time together. There's nothing like a common enemy to bring people together, and the rival school is the perfect enemy! Many small churches exist in areas where school rivalry is intense. And getting students to lay aside historical rivalries is not easy.

Similarly, kids from different communities often have a sense of loyalty to them. Sometimes this becomes an economic issue, too, but often just because of misperceptions regarding what people from other communities are like. In addition, districts might be competing with each other for funding and resources, and the conflict can be reproduced in the kids. For whatever reason, having a number of schools and communities represented in your small church youth group can cause problems.

There are, however, some ways to help ease the tension between students from rival schools and communities.

- Address the geographical problems early. Ignoring them will encourage the students to foster these divisions.
- Use the issue of loyalty to begin talking about where our true loyalties lie—with God, as opposed to things and people that aren't eternal.
- If the problem seems to be exacerbated by parents and other members of the community, bring it to the attention of your pastor.
- Accept that the students have developed social connections with people from the same schools and communities. This is okay, too—even healthy. It just shouldn't inhibit them from creating other connections as well.

- Respect and honor all of your kids' community and school traditions. If they believe you respect geographic differences, they might begin to also.
- Use crowdbreakers and activities that force kids to interact with one another.
- As much as possible, create youth group activities that meet in different homes. This changes everything!
- Be sure to follow up and encourage the "community momentum" after retreats, camps, and mission projects.

6

Havin' No Money Ain't So Funny

Why don't small churches spend more money on their youth?

In one year, a large-church pastor can make more than the entire annual budget of a small church. With this in mind, it's easier to understand why small churches have a hard time funding new programs. This is also the primary reason why not many small churches have paid youth workers, full or even part-time, and have to depend almost exclusively on volunteers. It also explains why there is very little money for youth ministry budgets.

"True followers of Christ expect the nation's network of Christian churches to ignite and sustain a moral and spiritual revolution. But successful revolutions take money. Although many Americans donate more than $50 billion to churches each year, the average ministry Outpost [e.g., a small church] is staked to just $120,000 to finance the local revolution. (In constant dollars, that is a 13 percent increase from the budget level in 1987, but still a relatively paltry bank account given the scope of the challenge.)"
—George Barna, *Boiling Point*

> **One small denomination I know of has an average of 40 to 50 congregants per church. In the entire denomination there's only a single part-time youth worker.**

One of the key differences between large churches and small churches in this situation is their financial outlook. Larger churches have an "investment mentality" whereas smaller churches have an "immediate results mentality." Large and megachurches tend to be governed by white-collar professionals. They come from a work culture that invests and waits for the big payoff later. Not so in the small church—it wants immediate results for its money and effort. A day's work means a day's wages. Therefore small churches may not be as ready to provide time and money for training and continuing education. If you spend money, church members should be able to see the benefits.

> **One in every five churches is without a full-time *pastor*.**

Because of their immediate results perspective, small churches may not understand or appreciate what is really necessary for effective youth ministry. The powers that be may believe the time and money needed is simply too high a price to pay. There are some ways, however, to introduce the "investment mentality" to your church:

- Present and articulate youth ministry as a "mission," not at all unlike groups from the church going overseas.
- Use metaphors the leaders can relate to (e.g., "You can't plant, tend to, and harvest crops in just one day, week—or even month. And when you do plant, there are no guarantees that anything will grow! You just know that you'll have to 'risk' planting something in order to get what you need to live. Effective youth ministry is no different.")
- Grow trust with your church board and pastor so you'll have the necessary credibility to make investments.

One year while I worked for a large church, I spent $1,500 on breakfast meetings with for students and leaders alone. At the end of the month, a woman from my church was behind me in line when I picked up my monthly tab. She happened to notice the amount of the bill. Without saying anything to me, she went straight to the church office administrator to express concern over the amount of money being spent. The administrator explained that we were using that time and money for "investing." The woman understood and had no other complaints.

Years later, when I was working for a small church, I had to get permission from the church board to be reimbursed for a restaurant tab of less than $10. What's more, it was also suggested that, in the future, I get permission before I spent any more money on "those kinds of activities."

Why don't many small church youth programs last long?

Once you're able to convince your church board to invest money and time in youth, you'll need to make sure you don't lose their trust. If the board members believe their investments aren't producing returns, they'll stop what they're doing—no different a scenario than if their farming methods aren't producing good crops. And if they cut off your funds, it'll be very difficult to ask for more in the future. Taking the following precautions can help prevent this disaster:

- Show and articulate results from the effort, time, and money spent. (Make sure you have this on paper.)
- Provide year-end reports that carefully explain what has been accomplished in the youth ministry because of the church's investment.
- Keep excellent financial records and be able to defend them well.
- Develop a clear and sensible plan for the program over the next year.

- Articulate your yearly plan and what you'll need to make it happen.
- Explain concisely the cost/benefit principle of your time and money: *It will cost this much to make these good things happen.*
- Manage your budget well.
- Know which purchases need preapproval (it might be all of them).
- Be prepared for the pastor and other committee members to have you ask wealthier members of the church to give money to the youth program.
- Plan fundraisers—but make sure your church approves them first.
- Don't let the limits on your resources paralyze you.

7

Building Blues and Tech-No!-Phobes

Two philosophies...

In some small churches, a chief concern is building maintenance—a practical, bottom-line mindset; in other small churches, a chief concern is turning the building into a museum—if kids break anything, they're in trouble!

Building Maintenance

Because many small churches struggle financially, they simply can't afford to maintain their buildings. Leaks get patched, but roofs don't get fixed; carpet holes get covered with furniture, but carpets don't get replaced. The fixes are quick and cheap, but rarely complete. This can make it difficult to find a comfortable and inviting room in which your kids can gather..

These building problems can make it difficult to do outreach. Your students could be embarrassed to invite their friends, and new students won't feel very comfortable. There are, however, some ways of dealing with this issue.

- Introduce your building concerns to the church board, and help them to understand that providing a safe, comfortable meeting place is an important part of youth ministry. Show how it fits into your ministry strategy—*ask*, don't *demand!*

> In addition to problems funding building maintenance, there can be problems funding things like extra hours of heat during the winter or air conditioning during the summer. There also may be unsafe parts of the building. Sometimes you can solve this problem by meeting outside, but that has a seasonal limit (unless you're working the middle school kids), and giving talks and lessons outside is usually not very effective.

- Ask other members or kids' parents if they have a room in which the youth group can meet one night a week (as long as the group doesn't get too big). A home is a very comfortable and safe place for kids.
- Request that one room in the church be reserved for youth group so your kids can fix and decorate it themselves. This is a great community-building project and will give the kids a sense of ownership.
- Use your creativity! Find ways to decorate a room temporarily (for a few hours) so that it will provide a sense of comfort.

> A number of years ago, when I was a youth pastor at a small church, none of the students was interested in meeting in the oversized church basement painted Pepto-Bismol pink and filled with broken furniture. To make meetings more interesting, I decided to take the four to six regular attendees to the local fast-food joint for our Bible study. They loved it! It wasn't long, however, before I heard an elder and his wife were disturbed and believed that I should not leave the church for Bible study. I had violated their traditional belief that "the Lord's work ought to be done in the Lord's house." Meeting at a fast-food joint for a Bible study is a method that any good, self-respecting Young Life leader would use. But this small church had its own beliefs and attachments to its buildings. There are always obstacles, but you can't give up being creative.

Remember: In order to attract new students, it's important to offer them something as least as good as what they get at home or school. This can be most difficult when it comes to comfort. If your building is substandard and outdated, then you'll have a hard time getting their friends to return.

Building Preservation

Another building problem can arise because some small churches are concerned with preservation. Members are afraid to allow kids in rooms. Kids can wear out new carpet and paint very fast.

However, many congregations work hard at making their buildings museums for the chosen instead of sanctuaries for the broken and lost. This is an unfortunate problem—and these churches may be difficult to change. Often those concerned with unreasonable building preservation are older church families—and it's likely that they're more interested in keeping up appearances than anything else. For many of them, the church building is their greatest achievement. In other cases, the big spenders in the church will be concerned with keeping "their" building from harm, and fighting them might mean a loss of funding

I once worked at a small church where part of my job was to reach out to the neighborhood kids. One evening I noticed that a bunch of kids from the neighborhood were meeting on a flat section of the churchyard to play football. "It can't get any better than this!" I thought. I got out of the car, met them, and played a little football. Over the next few weeks this became a regular practice...until the grass began to disappear and the special light bulb behind the 18-year-old aluminum cross went out. This became a major subject at the very next board meeting. Clearly, at least to some of the board members, the kids were responsible for the light bulb. And who could argue against the reason the grass was so bare? From that point on, I was strongly "encouraged" to play football with the neighborhood kids somewhere else. I tried, but the move changed the chemistry of the group and the whole thing died—all because of a light bulb and some dead grass.

for the youth. This may not be a hill worth dying on, so you will have to choose your battles. Here are some tips:

- Ask some of the kids' parents if they'd be willing to host the group once a week. If this is too much to ask, see if once a month with a house rotation would work.
- Scout other possible meeting locations. Nearby community centers, schools, or restaurants might provide workable alternatives.
- Present your group's needs to the church board, and ask the members to come up with some ideas. If you aren't involved in this process, though, you might get stuck with a solution that doesn't quite work.
- Ask the church board for one room dedicated to the youth. This might make the kids feel like they are being cast aside and given the dregs, but it can also become their own place—a sanctuary away from the adults.

> Sometimes getting past the board members who make it their personal calling to protect the building from any and all "creative ministry" experiences can be more daunting than having no building at all.

Why don't small churches use the latest technology?

Unfortunately, most small churches can't afford high-priced multimedia equipment. In fact, the primary multimedia device is still the flannel graph board, with an occasional overhead projector, complete with a loud, cranky cooling fan.

But another reason behind their antiquated technology is their perspective. I worked at one small church in which the secretary was expected to copy 100 bulletins on a copier that produced a page about every 5 seconds. Church elders wouldn't let her purchase a new one, because, after all, years ago the former secretary used a stenograph.

Not understanding how the culture has changed and that technology could help the church grow, the elders simply couldn't approve the cost. Many small churches share this same attitude toward technology—they are technophobes. They often can't understand that producing things like quality literature and newsletters will attract people.

Here are some problems you may face:

- Technologically astute students might not enjoy your low-tech meetings.
- You might have to use or purchase your own sound systems, computers, projection screens, or other equipment.
- Older and more conservative church members might disapprove of movie projection and sound systems.
- Using technology might create tension between the congregation and the youth group.

Although these can be sticky issues, there are ways to deal with them. A few tips:

- Learn to use your resources—borrow or ask for donations from church members who are a bit more technologically aware and can afford it.
- Check with other neighborhood churches—they might have equipment they're willing to share.
- Gain support from the younger adults in the congregation—they can stand up for your technological cause in congregational meetings.
- Subscribe to some of the more helpful and technologically aware youth ministry magazines—and supported by the Billy Graham Association and Focus on the Family, organizations your older church members are likely to revere and respect—making these available to parents and others so you can introduce new technological ideas in less threatening ways
- Discuss in your parent and congregational meetings how you want to study technology and pop culture with the youth—this can be a disarming way of introducing them to the idea that understanding these forces is a great way to reach kids and encourage their spiritual growth.

- Learn to include certain aspects of technology that are acceptable to most of the congregation when you give presentations—over time, they will become more comfortable with it, and you will be able to introduce more.

8

Calling All Volunteers!

In the small church, with so much reliance on volunteers, youth group leaders can take any form—from the head pastor to concerned parents, from new members to college students who attended the group while in high school. In some cases, retired grandparents might be running the program.

Still, pastors and church administrators must choose youth leaders carefully. If there's no one capable of working well and effectively with students, the church might think about spending its resources on other ministries and involving kids in those. There might even be other youth groups the kids can attend. Recognizing these options will benefit the youth.

But if it's within the small church's resources to develop a youth program, the following tips will be helpful:

- Make certain that adult volunteers have a genuine calling to work with students.
- Be willing to recruit, subsidize training for, and make resources available to potential youth leaders. (There are many fairly inexpensive resources.)
- Be willing to develop a program that will help your kids who happen to attend other youth groups deal with potential differences between the doctrines of both churches.

- Make sure kids are connected to other Christians of their own ages; *they need a Christian community as much as adults do.*
- Be open to recruiting leaders from nearby colleges.

Avoid desperate measures. Just because any old adult is willing to volunteer doesn't mean that adult should have anything to do with the youth ministry.

Why do many small churches have a number of different youth leaders?

In the majority of small churches, the pastor is the only paid minister. Indeed, the pastor may be one of the few parishioners with a college degree. This is another reason why many small churches depend on volunteers. Since most volunteers have other jobs and obligations, they generally can only offer only about five to 10 hours a week. But it's almost impossible to develop a youth program in a 10-hours-per-week window. Thus many churches have a number of different volunteers running the youth program.

Even in churches with paid youth workers, limited resources might mean that volunteers are often called upon to assist with planning, budgeting, and offering meeting space. All these volunteers are involved in leadership, and many develop relationships with the kids. Although having a number of volunteers is beneficial in some respects, it can also create tensions.

Whether you volunteer as the head youth worker or serve with a group volunteers in a small church youth ministry, it's important to be aware of the following:

- Because volunteers normally have less time to develop relationships with students than paid youth workers, their results will not be as dramatic or as visible.
- Because it's difficult for youth workers with limited time to develop relationships, it's also easier for them to fall into the trap of spending time programming for rather than *interacting with youth.* This trap must be avoided!

- Because students might not be able to see the same leader at every meeting, their level of comfort with a group of leaders can be diminished or underdeveloped.
- Because it's difficult for volunteers to spend a lot of time with kids, they don't often feel as if they have the right to ask important questions about the kids' lives.
- Because many leaders are volunteers, they often don't have the experience or training to deal with difficult situations.
- However, because they aren't getting paid to talk about God and spend time with the kids, volunteers can speak and relate to kids with more authority.

Why do many small church youth workers burn out?

In his book *Small Strong Churches*, Kennon L. Callahan notes that because small churches have limited resources to accomplish the same tasks as more affluent, larger churches, a number of problems are created. In some cases, important programs get left behind because there's no funding for them. Conversely, some small churches attempt to spread what resources they do have among several church-related programs within the community.

If the youth program isn't a church's priority, that church's government will likely make sure that other programs are adequately funded and resourced before they think in the slightest about the youth program's needs. If they're honest about this, they might be willing to help their youth workers sit down with other churches that have strong programs.

What's more, if the church leadership doesn't prioritize its ministries very well, those involved in youth work could also be asked to help in other areas. Similarly the kids themselves might be expected to spend a significant amount of time working in other areas of the church. Unfortunately this limits time you can spend developing the youth program, as well as all of the church's other ministries. When volun-

> **Ask yourself whether you're in youth ministry because you feel God has called you or because it seemed like a good way to get involved.**

teers are spread between three or four different ministries—and unable to really focus on any one of them—all the programs suffer. And if youth workers are involved in too many other ministries, the kids will suffer, too.

Here are some tips to help youth workers stay sane:

- Learn to say "no" to your church's additional requests for your time and talents so you have time and energy for planning—and for the kids.
- Remind the pastor and other leaders about the limits on resources so they don't make commitments the church can't achieve.
- Make sure your job description clearly outlines your responsibilities and **stick to them**.
- Learn all you can about time management and organizational skills to maximize your efficiency.
- Make the time to meet with other youth workers in similar positions as yourself so you can offer each other support and encouragement.
- Learn to celebrate the small accomplishments, because much of the time, what may seem like small achievements are really very big in the small church setting.
- Don't compare your youth programs to others, especially those with more resources.
- Be fair to yourself and evaluate your youth ministry program according to criteria relevant to your situation.

> **In many cases it will be better, and healthier, for a small church to send its kids to a nearby youth group.**

9
Keep Your Chin Up

Why aren't I getting the same results as other youth workers?

I once heard a well-known pastor say, "Ninety percent of the pastors in this country ought to get out of the ministry." (This would be just about all of the small churches.) It was his belief that this 90 percent can't minister effectively. Although he may have had all sorts of reasons for that percentage, it seems he really meant that those pastors didn't do ministry *his* way and were getting *his* results—which makes their ministry invalid. Of course, this simply isn't true. This kind of arrogance has been one of the single most destructive barriers to youth ministry in the small church.

Many small church youth workers sense this prevailing attitude and it can cause significant problems. And when small church youth workers feel "not as good," they can become ineffective—a self-fulfilling prophecy. Remember, different ministry contexts have different problems and produce different results. That's what I tried to emphasize in the first section of this book. If youth workers can stop playing the deadly comparison game, over half the battle—in terms of reaching kids effectively—would be won.

Why am I overwhelmed?

There are so many reasons small churches are small, and each reason means you have to create a different approach to youth ministry. It's important that, as a small church youth worker, *you give yourself permission to so things differently.* I hope the first section of this book has added to your insight regarding ministry context. Recognizing differences is the first step in managing your youth program. In fact, in any sort of ministry, determining the context is vital for success.

But you can't overlook your attitude or the church's. If you or your church expect too much from the youth group, then it won't succeed. Each church context is different, just as each youth ministry context is different—and, therefore, expectations. You must realize this—as does your church. Being overwhelmed by outrageous expectations can create harmful attitudes of failure and worthlessness.

> **Make sure your expectations for the youth group match your ministry context.**

Why do I feel inadequate?

Remember, bigger isn't always better. Sometimes the most effective ministry is done in small groups or one-on-one. Some of the biggest spiritual breakthroughs I've witnessed have come through small groups. Although large groups and outreach are important, the impact of developing personal relationships with kids will last longer than a talk at a meeting with 100 kids.

If you're uncertain whether you're doing well, talk with other small church youth workers. They can offer support and candid evaluation based on your ministry context, not someone else's. If you're trying to do youth ministry in a church that's fighting your program, then it probably won't succeed—but that's not your fault!

As it's helped you identify your ministry context, this first section should also have helped you pinpoint some of the problems plaguing small church your ministry. Just knowing that these problems exist due to the nature of the beast (and not because you're inadequate) is hopefully an encouragement.

Which way do I go?

Once you've established your ministry context and established a healthy attitude, then you need to start developing your program. Of course, each program will be different because it's based on what you've discovered about yourself, your kids, and your church. The next section offers different models of ministry. Different models work better in different situations, so be prepared to start picking and choosing your specific context.

In *The Church Staff Handbook*, Harold J. Westing notes, "The process of our ministry is spiritual reproduction, not spiritual addition." (2 Timothy 2:2) The following illustration explains what he means further:

Let's suppose it takes two years to help one grow spiritually to where he or she can reproduce also. Then if you were to invest your life in another, there will be:

Let's suppose you lead one person to Christ each day, but by doing this, you don't have time to help them grow. Then there will be:

After 2 Years	
2 mature Christians	731 Converts

After 4 Years	
4 mature Christians	1,462 Converts

After 10 Years	
32 mature Christians	3,653 Converts

After 20 Years	
1,024 mature Christians	7,306 Converts

After 30 Years	
32,768 mature Christians	10,958 Converts

Bottom line? The Great Commission calls youth workers to make *disciples*, not just converts.

Models That'll Fit to a "T"

Four Approaches to Youth Ministry in the Small Church

10
Building the Right Kingdom

Not long ago, I had a conversation with a young, very talented youth worker who enthusiastically shared a "new model" for youth ministry. The basic idea was to blitz kids with incredible audio-visual technology. They planned to use this state-of-the-art technology, an essential staple of adolescent culture, redemptively—to use it for God instead of against him.

It became clear that he believed this technological model was the wave of the future for all youth programs. After listening to him for a while, I told him I thought the model was a great one for his church. But I added that it wouldn't work well in the average church. Because the average church is small, it really couldn't afford the costs, not to mention the inefficiency of using all that equipment for only 10 to 15 kids.

What is a youth ministry model?

Simply put, a youth ministry model is a prescribed approach to operating a youth program. It offers an outline of specific goals, ideas, techniques, and methods to help young adults get to know God and develop an intimate, ongoing relationship with Christ. An awareness of different youth ministry models can be helpful for anyone working in youth ministry.

But discussing and deciding which models to use can paralyze small church youth workers. Even once they've discovered their ministry context and developed healthy ministry attitudes, they still can have a hard time deciding which models to use and how to implement them.

What models are the right models?

For years, youth ministry has been dominated with the belief that if a youth worker uses the right model, she can have a "successful" program. Unfortunately, some people still believe this, and it harms the ways in which they approach their ministry. The belief that there is "right model" for all youth programs stems from these two statements:

1. *The right kind of model will help* **me** *build a kingdom.*
2. *The model works in his church, so it can work in mine.*

Building the Right Kingdom

Often, personal and institutional ambition can be the motivation for choosing certain models or approaches to ministry. Unfortunately many pastors and youth workers see church ministry as *their* ministry, not God's. In other words, the more people they get, the more *they* are doing to build a kingdom. (It sounds a little like the disciples fighting over who would get to sit next to Jesus, huh?) Because of this attitude, the number of students involved becomes the primary manner for evaluating a youth ministry program's effectiveness. Although this is a problem for all youth workers, "numbers" can be a particularly sensitive issue.

Remember your approach to youth ministry should reflect your ministry context. You are there for the kids, not for the program or the individual church. Any motivation other than this can spell disaster. In fact, many small churches are perfectly suited for types of ministries that do not involve large numbers—ministries that develop mature *disciples* rather than many *converts*.

When teaching my college kids, I make a distinction between *a kingdom* and *the Kingdom*. When youth workers strive to develop "a kingdom," he is using the ministry to build his personal, little ministry empire—to get a lot of converts. Conversely, when a person works toward developing "The Kingdom," he is working for God—to develop mature disciples. (There's more about the difference between the two in the chapter, "Success: Ministry Outcomes.")

If a youth worker believes there's only one right model for youth ministry, he probably wants to develop *a kingdom* through a program that can be evaluated based on outward appearances. A youth worker who realizes her approach to youth ministry will vary depending on the needs of her kids is probably working hard toward building *the Kingdom* through a program that's judged by what's written on the hearts of its disciples. (Sound familiar?)

> **Stop judging by mere appearances, and make a right judgment.**
> **—*John 7:24***

Create Your Own Model

I've spent many lunches with discouraged, frustrated youth workers, volunteer and paid, who were tripped up by the belief that there's only one right model for youth ministry. Often it would take me hours to convince them that the only *right* model is the model they create by tailoring approaches to their specific ministry contexts, gifts, and calling.

Indeed, there are many youth workers who've done fantastic jobs in their churches and communities. They probably have a lot of insight to share and advice to offer colleagues who work in churches like theirs. **But their successes don't qualify them to speak about youth ministry in every context.** I've had experiences in large and small churches in small towns and suburbia. Although I can speak about *universal principles* of youth ministry and intuitively guess what might work in a particular church, any success that I've experienced doesn't

> It is important not to be intimidated by the successes and marketing of those who peddle universal models of ministry. A model is often more stumbled upon than strategically realized, and rarely do we get to see the dark side of the evolutionary process.
>
> ——Chap Clark,
> *Starting Right: Thinking Theologically about Youth Ministry*

qualify me to speak about how to do youth ministry in urban churches, ethnic churches, or foreign countries.

How do I choose which ministry model to use in my ministry context?

Unfortunately, many previously successful youth workers fail when they change churches because they try to apply the model they used in their last church to their new one. Practically, most youth ministries work best when they adapt a few ideas from a number of different

> Any honest, successful youth worker who's been around a while will tell you, tongue in cheek, that he steals what he can and cans what he steals. He makes it a habit to find specific methods and techniques that can be inserted into his own ministry model. He may not use the idea right away—he may can it for a while—but he's able to use it when it'll work.

models. And although it's helpful to know which models to use, it's probably easier to determine your approach and build your own model based on a number of others.

If your ministry context will work well to build disciples, then—keeping in mind that you're using the discipleship approach—you would develop a model using small group Bible studies, leadership meetings, and large youth group meetings. If your ministry context calls for the inclusive congregational approach, then you would probably want to use parts of a ministry model that incorporate kids into the worship service.

> Models are developed out of a response to a unique setting and need . . . Few start-up pioneers began with a vision to change the world. The seeds were planted in response to a unique need and setting, and the founding group moved on from there . . . This is important because today most ministry leaders either do not trust themselves to create something from scratch in response to a given setting or need, or are not even willing to take the time to ask hard questions. It is simply easier to trust the "experts."
>
> —Chap Clark,
> *Starting Right: Thinking Theologically about Youth Ministry*

How do I know which youth ministry approach will best help me develop my own model?

Being aware of your ministry context is the first step in developing a model for your program. Ministry context and personal comfort determine which approach will work well in your church. As you read through this section, write down or mark any ideas that seem like they might work for your church, your youth group, one of your small groups, or even one or two of your kids.

There are so many different models and approaches that it would be difficult for to list and describe them all in this book. I have included, however, three approaches which seem to fit most small churches. These are the inclusive congregational approach, the discipleship

> In *Images of the Church in the New Testament,* Paul Minear lists the different church and ministry models depicted in the New Testament. There are 96! Even the members of the first church realized that effective ministry took many forms.
>
> While no youth program should ever neglect outreach and evangelism, most small churches are limited in their ability to reach students in schools and communities. Therefore, their primary task will be to focus on the students they have and how best to serve them. This requires a different approach to planning your program.

approach, and the mentoring approach. In addition, I have included a chapter, "Alternative Approaches," for small churches that might not have a typical small-church mentality. Using any or all of these approaches enables youth workers to develop multiple models for almost any small church setting.

11

The Inclusive Congregational Approach: An Extended Family

Recently I had an opportunity to preach in a small church in Western Pennsylvania. As the service began, I noted with great interest that the worship leaders were a group of five teenagers, each about 15 or 16 years old. I marveled as they confidently led the multigenerational congregation, joyfully playing old, established hymns as well as modern-day praise songs. Later in the service, another group of teenagers took up the offering; one young teenager, on her own initiative, corralled an out-of-control little girl during the children's sermon, and an adolescent boy took responsibility for adjusting the lighting during another part of the service. The youth were leading and leading well.

Here is a small church that includes its students, regularly, during the most sensitive day of the week for the church. This is a church determined to include the youth in its life and ministry. In other words, the whole church is responsible for the development of its kids.

> There are many small churches that, although they sympathize with the needs of the students, nevertheless believe "teenagers should be seen but not heard." The inclusive congregational approach probably won't work in these churches.

What does the inclusive congregational approach look like?

Responsibility for the youth doesn't need to be compartmentalized or delegated to a paid youth worker or a volunteer. The church can surround its youth and do whatever is necessary to nurture them and participate in their Christian development. In *Four Views of Youth Ministry and the Church,* Malan Nel writes, "The Inclusive

> Young people are not just partly the congregation's responsibility, they are wholly so. The essence of God's dealings and relationship with people—and especially with those in the community of believers—makes such a distinction indefensible.
>
> —Malan Nel,
> *Four Views of Youth Ministry and the Church*

Congregational Approach, therefore, is more about finding a place for children and adolescents than about dreaming up new modes of ministry." He also notes what this approach looks like in a church:

- The congregation is concerned about the spiritual needs of the whole church—youth and adults.
- Youth are not neglected or ignored.
- Youth are the congregation's responsibility, not merely the responsibility of the youth worker.

> Youth ministry is not about finding an extra place for yet another ministry, but about finding a place for youth within every ministry.
>
> —Malan Nel,
> *Four Views of Youth Ministry and the Church*

What should I do if the inclusive congregational approach fits my church?

I can think of no better way for a healthy and motivated small church to do its youth ministry than through this approach. But, again, it's important that the church is *healthy* and *motivated*. While totally healthy churches (large or small) are relatively rare, many small churches and their youth workers simply don't have the confidence or congregational support to take this approach. Many adults in these congregations are interested in youth only if they act like them, and they also believe it's too much trouble to change the way ministry is done.

Nevertheless, more so than any other kind of church, the small church is the most open to the inclusive congregational approach— largely because it needs help with additional leadership and because the kids tend to be less busy than those from larger churches. If you believe your church will be open to this kind of approach, here are some things to consider:

- The entire congregation must be involved; if there are groups in the congregation that don't want to include youth, the approach— will not work.
- Including students in the total life of the congregation can't mean giving students the jobs no one else wants.
- The congregation, adults and teenagers, will need to be patient during the time it takes for the kids to learn and get comfortable with their new responsibilities.
- Students must be allowed to fail without being scolded or lectured. (After all, are adults scolded or lectured when *they* are learning new jobs?)
- Youth workers must be responsible for recruiting, training, and helping students learn their jobs.
- Youth workers must intercede between youth and adults when there are problems.

> The inclusive congregational model of youth ministry isn't as appealing to large churches because of their tremendous emphasis on "professionalism."

What are some ways I can build the inclusive congregational approach into my model of youth ministry?

One of the best ways in which this approach can be used is to involve families. Making families stronger and better able to minister to their own kids is a great thing, and it helps develop the church community,

> Never forget that families have the most significant effect on the spiritual development of teenagers.

too. While some might think this is a bit naïve and quaint, it's actually the kind of thing that happens when parents choose to home school their kids. Parents become role models, mentors, and advisors. This is perfect because kids spend a lot of time with their parents.

As the families in the church each become stronger, there will be

- 24 percent of teenage Christians say they converted after a conversation with a family member.
- 14 percent of teenage Christians were raised in a Christian home.
- 47 percent of teenage Christians say their parents have the greatest influence on their spiritual development.
- 43 percent of teenage Christians talk daily to family or friends about spiritual things.
- 70 percent of teenage Christians have daily conversations with their mothers about important issues in their lives, and 53 percent have similar conversations with their fathers.

—from a report by George Barna

stronger relationships between families, too, and the number of role models, mentors, and advisors will grow—it is an extended family!

Whether or not kids are comfortable admitting it, the family continues to have a substantial impact on their lives. This isn't something we should ignore or deemphasize, no matter what youth ministry approaches we use or model we create. This should also offer some real encouragement to those small churches that depend primarily on family involvement. Here are some ways you can involve families in your ministry:

- Target parents and families throughout the year, offering meetings and chances for family participation in services.
- Include family ministry as part of the Sunday school curriculum for adult and youth classes.
- Invite experts to speak at church regarding family ministry.
- Address the needs of families with young children and teenagers.

Have whole families usher, greet, hand out bulletins, read the call to worship, lead music in worship, or participate in some other aspect of the service.

What are some ministry areas in which students can participate?

Knowing where and how to involve youth can be tricky. A shy kid probably won't be good at reading the call to worship or singing during the offering (although she might surprise you). But most churches have ministry holes they need to fill, and asking youth to help is an excellent idea. As long as you and the students feel as though the job is one they can handle—and the congregation supports it—give it a shot. (Even adults who offer to do jobs in the church sometimes fail because they aren't ready.)

Find out what each kid's talents are, and use them.

Every church has different ministries, programs, and needs—so you'll have to develop your model based on this truth. Here are some jobs your students might be able to do:

- Help with sound during services and special events—some are technologically aware and know how to use the equipment.
- Lead or participate in music during services or special events— some kids might prefer contemporary songs to the hymns most church members like, so move carefully on this one.
- Read the call to worship.
- Take the offering.
- Assist in the nursery.
- Help teach Sunday school classes for younger kids.
- Help in the church office.
- Help cook church dinners.
- Help with church maintenance.

12

The Discipleship Approach

What is discipleship?

In the early church, and for centuries after, discipleship was a process that trained and enabled Christians to take on the spiritual disciplines of the Christian faith. It was these disciplines, they believed, that helped to develop a spiritually mature Christian.

Unfortunately, the current meaning and practice of "discipleship" is much more narrow. Today many believe discipleship is "managing and avoiding sin in one's life." So discipleship has become a series of devotions, immersion in fellowship, and avoiding "the world."

Clearly, the practice of personal devotions, fostering solid Christian relationships, and keeping our minds and hearts protected from corruption are important. But they don't encompass all it means to be a Christian in the world. Really, discipleship should have to do with the fascination, discovery, and experience of God. But because discipleship is now equated with simply doing the "right things," many church

> ...discipleship...<u>trains</u> students to be God's people in an ungodly world, <u>equipped</u> with Bible study and prayer skills developed in a <u>caring atmosphere</u> with a view to <u>reproducing</u> their Christian lives in others.
> —Mark Senter III, *Reaching a Generation for Christ*

leaders have begun to use the term "spiritual formation" to express the essence of discipleship—the development of a mature Christian.

> One of Satan's greatest victories has been convincing Christians that all they really need to do in order to grow in their faith is to maintain a devotional life.
> But often we trade the devoted life for the devotional life. And this trade-off is being passed on to our students. The devotional life isn't bad; it's just not all there is to the process of maturing and growing as a Christian. The devoted life demands that everything we do is an act of devotion to Christ. The devotional life, on the other hand, is often used simply to help us manage our sin or provide short-term, often shallow, inspiration.

How do I know if the discipleship approach is right for my church and youth group?

Any church that wants to take a discipleship approach to designing its model for youth ministry needs to be prepared to make changes. Youth workers will have to commit themselves to a new kind of depth in their own faith.

But if leaders don't develop their relationships with Jesus, then their kids won't want to develop theirs, either. After all, people can't give what they haven't got. If you aren't willing to live way beyond 20-minute devotionals, simplistic rules for Christian living, church attendance, and fast-food theology, then you really have nothing more to offer students who want to mature spiritually.

There is no biblical way that we can live our faith without significant sacrifices and making truly hard choices. When students see this, it will make a difference in their lives. Anything that's "formed"—spiritually or otherwise—involves stretching and molding. These aren't easy and can include some soreness. But if you and your church are up for the challenge, your small church is in an excellent position to take a discipleship approach to youth ministry.

Truthfully, discipleship is more natural in small churches than in large ones. Brutally honest evaluation is easier between students and leaders when they are comfortable and familiar with one another. In large churches, these relationships are often harder to develop. Although the discipleship approach works well in small churches, it works best in groups with at least 20 students because small groups should be formed to help with spiritual development in different areas. Having competent adult leaders is more important than numbers, though. (The discipleship approach can be adapted into a model for groups with smaller numbers, but the leaders can't be adapted.)

> **If you always do what you've always done, then you'll always get what you've always gotten.**

Believe it or not, our postmodern culture is producing young men and women who are increasingly hungry for what used to be the regular spiritual disciplines of the Christian faith. Increasingly turned off by the easy, feel-good faith that saturates large portions of the current Christian community, these teenagers are looking for deeper and more profound ways to experience God.

> **Do you not know that in a race all the runners run, but only one gets the prize? Run in such a way as to get the prize. Everyone who competes in the games goes into strict training. They do it to get a crown that will not last; but we do it to get a crown that will last forever. Therefore I do not run like a man running aimlessly; I do not fight like a man beating the air. No, I beat my body and make it my slave so that after I have preached to others, I myself will not be disqualified for the prize.**
>
> **—1 Corinthians 9:24-27**

What are some ways I can use a discipleship approach to develop my model of youth ministry?

Small church youth workers would benefit from researching the various program models that are formed from the discipleship approach. There are a number of "discipleship models" available, and they can be adapted for almost any ministry context. One of the most common is the Son Life model that offers multiple training seminars throughout the year. In addition, organizations like Youth Specialties and Group offer conventions, seminars, and training materials for models based on the discipleship approach.

The discipleship approach works best when you can form your kids into small groups, as well as one large group. This allows for intimacy, comfort, accountability, and fellowship. In *Reaching a Generation for Christ*, Mark Senter III lists a number of key ingredients for using discipleship in models of youth ministry. Below is a list I compiled from his, and I have included other comments and suggestions, too. (Here, as with other suggestions, use what works with your group.)

Core Group Meetings

Discipleship works best when an intimate group of students can share, explore, and process their faith. It has to be a "safe place" where the leader and kids experience real Christian community. The value of these kinds of experiences cannot be overemphasized. The real power of the Christian faith is the experience of truth in the midst of authentic relationships lived out incarnationally—particularly by leaders.

A core group also gives those students a sense of belonging. Although they all belong to the youth group or church, when they have intimate friendships formed with leaders and other students, they feel responsible for and to the others with whom they have developed

lose relationships. Here are some ways to begin developing core
roups:

Recruit small groups of students with things in common.

Make sure the members of each group have similar school calendars.

Keep your core groups at six to eight students; anything more than
that and the sense of intimacy is lost.

Keep the groups the same gender so young men and women have
an opportunity to more openly share gender-specific issues that are
so much a part of teenagers' lives.

Insist on a covenant of confidentiality between all group members—what is said in the group stays in the group—so it's a safe
place.

**The larger the group, the more nonverbal communication there is.
This disrupts verbal and relational communication. Kirkpatrick
Sale illustrates the huge increase of the number of signals that a
leader will have to manage, as the group gets larger:**

Two kids = two nonverbal signals going back and forth
Three kids = nine nonverbal signals going back and forth
Four kids = 28 nonverbal signals going back and forth
Five kids = 75 nonverbal signals going back and forth
Six kids = 186 nonverbal signals going back and forth
Seven kids = 441 nonverbal signals going back and forth
Eight kids = 1,016 nonverbal signals going back and forth
Nine kids = 2,295 nonverbal signals going back and forth
Ten kids = 5,110 nonverbal signals going back and forth

arge Group Meetings

addition to core groups, students also need large or combined group
ctivities to create powerful worship experiences and to broaden their
hristian fellowship. This is also a great opportunity for students to
ke ownership of their program through various leadership roles such
playing in the worship band, running the sound system, setting up
d cleaning up, or leading discussion groups following the talk. One
ossibility is that each core group is responsible for one part of the large
eeting.

If your large group has 15 to 20 kids, consider meeting in a church member's or kid's parents' family room. This might be difficult (especially for urban churches, where meeting at night in some neighborhoods is unsafe; and rural churches, where long-distance travel in winter can be dangerous), but if it's possible, it can have some great benefits. For students in small churches, meeting in homes can help foster intimacy and community, even in the large group meetings.

Here are some tips for planning large group meetings:

- Plan the entire school year in advance. Should the schedule not work, you can revise it whenever you need to, but having a set schedule makes it easier for the kids and parents to include church meetings in their plans.
- Always publish and mail (or hand out) your schedule so parents and kids know when and where the group is meeting. If they miss week or two, they'll still have a calendar to remind them.
- Always notify the whole group of any changes—i.e., send out mailings. It isn't any fun if a kid shows up for the first time in two months only to find there isn't youth group on that night any more
- Insist that the large group demonstrate sensitivity to and respect fo your meeting place, wherever it is. Larger groups can sometimes ge unruly, so addressing it early is important.

Leadership Group Meetings

Small group leaders (both students and adults) need to meet to plan and discuss the discipleship goals and results of the small and large groups. They also need to encourage and counsel one another. But thi should *never* be a "gossip session." Rather, it should be a time during which small group leaders share the joys and frustrations of leadership

Leadership group meetings should take place weekly. It's helpful to have them before or after other meetings in the same place so leaders aren't pushed for time. As with every meeting, include prayer. Leaders and students need it, too. Here are some issues that should be discusse in leadership groups:

- **The calendar**—confirm times and locations of all events.
- **Roles**—confirm the different jobs the adult and student leaders have at each activity.
- **All activities from the week before**—evaluate them so that what worked can be used again and what didn't work can be shelved.
- **New training**—this is a great time to instill new ideas and offer further instruction in leadership skills.
- **Individual needs and concerns**—pray for the groups, the leaders, and the students, and find out how the needs can be met.
- **God**—have a devotional time in which leaders read Scripture or pray for each other.

Camps, Retreats, and Big Events

Outside-the-church experiences can help students become an essential part of a strong discipleship program. As well as offering student leaders an opportunity to grow, camps, retreats, and big events can attract church youth who are not active in youth group. They also can help create turning points in students' lives. These activities offer chances to have "mountaintop experiences," times when students feel the immediate presence of God. These moments remain with kids—and they'll help them remember why they made a commitment to God and the church in the first place.

There are some benefits from and problems with camps, retreats, and other events. But many problems can be managed beforehand, and, if you're prepared, the benefits can be great. Here are some ideas for when you're planning any big event:

- Network with other churches and ministries, large and small, that can provide resources unimaginable to the average small church.
- Plan six months to a year in advance so students and parents can get the events on their calendars and begin to save money.
- Have fundraisers or scholarship programs in place ahead of time so students who wouldn't otherwise be able to go can plan ahead, too.
- Hold debriefing meetings to maximize the effect that camps, retreats and events may have had on your kids.

What leaders will I need for the discipleship approach?

Mark Senter III says that in order to have discipleship as a part of your program, you need strong leaders. Although they'll develop their skills as they use them, these students must already have a commitment to developing their own spiritual maturity. Leaders can be trained, and should be. In fact, many of your student leaders will have been kids who've been coming to youth group for a few years already. They have been "in training" since day one.

Adults can also be trained. Some might be volunteers for a while before they're ready to disciple kids, and some will take longer than others to mature enough to become leaders. All leaders must be chosen wisely, though. Remember, just because someone feels like it'd be a good idea to try to lead a group doesn't mean that person will be a good fit. The kids come first, even if it means hurting an adult's ego.

Here's a list of leaders you may need:

1. **Youth pastor/youth worker**. The primary communicator between and administrator for student small groups. (Although leadership can be shared, there should be one person on whom a final or critical decision rests.)
2. **Core group leader**. Primary leader of a small group who has committed to his students long-term. (It's helpful to have two leaders per group so one can be used as a backup in case of a family emergency, job transfer, or other unforeseen event.)
3. **Student leader**. Responsible for leading some part of the large group meeting or assisting adult leaders in core groups. (Providing kids with leadership opportunities is vital to helping them grow spiritually.)
4. **Parents**. Assist with certain activities and events or donate time to working with kids. (Because parents are such an important and prominent part of kids' lives, it's crucial to involve parents in their kids' spiritual growth.)

13

The Mentoring Approach

How will I know if I should consider using a mentoring approach?

There's a great need for Christian adults to invest in students' lives. In the same way, students should to learn what it means to invest in each other. Spiritual mentoring in youth ministry means the intentional investment in a student or small group to help other students mature in their relationships with Christ. The ultimate goal is every student's spiritual formation.

Whereas discipleship focuses on helping groups of students develop skills and giving them tools they need to become mature Christians, mentoring is all about one-on-one relationships. Mentors guide students; they offer insight when teenagers face difficult situations and advice when they need help. Also, mentors model what it means to be a mature Christian. Students will not mature spiritually without a steadfast commitment from adults to instruct, motivate, and inspire them.

The greatest resource the small church has to offer its students is meaningful, faith-drenched relationships.

> The strength of the small church is its ability to create, nurture, and build relationships in an intimate setting. While many small churches may struggle to produce a formal youth ministry program, many of them can mentor quite well.

What does a mentoring approach to youth ministry look like?

In a church where I had been working for a short time, there was a group of high school guys who hung out together all of the time. As their new youth pastor, I was still getting to know them, so I invited one of the guys from that group, Phil, to meet me for breakfast before school. He eagerly agreed, so we met at one of the local greasy spoons for pancakes and an omelet.

I arrived at 6 a.m., and Phil was already there. We sat down and talked a bit about grades, sports, and then girls. Sensing that he wanted to go deeper on this last topic, I began asking probing, open-ended, sometimes humorous, questions. Nervously at first, and then with more confidence, Phil was able to share with me that he didn't have a girlfriend, but that he certainly did have a strong sex drive that caused him to think things he didn't what to think, say things he wished he hadn't said, visit places on the Internet he was embarrassed to have seen, and do things he didn't want to do. In addition, he shared that a number of his friends struggled with the same issues.

I asked him what he thought he needed to do about this problem and what we could do to help his friends. At first he shrugged his shoulders, looked down at the table, and said he wasn't sure. But after

> Before going off to fight a 10-year war against the Trojans, Odysseus entrusted his young son, Telemachus, to a wise friend, Mentor, to be educated and trained in Greek customs and practices. After running into some trouble, Odysseus returned instead 20 years later and discovered that Telemachus was a mature and accomplished man. Mentor had guided Telemachus as he grew and matured. This is the origin of our word *mentor*.

few minutes, he said some kind of accountability could be helpful.

Before we concluded breakfast, I asked Phil if he would be open to meeting on a regular basis, not only for accountability, but also to develop our friendship and talk about other important areas of his life. He was. In addition, we made arrangements to meet with his friends. He agreed to get them together and propose a mentoring accountability group. Phil said, "We need an adult who can help us with these kinds of things because we just can't do it alone." I was willing to help, but I also asked, "Do I have your permission to ask you difficult questions and enter, as a friend, into all the areas of your life?" He wanted this, so we established a mentoring relationship. This is the essence of the covenant agreement—and it must work for the covenant to survive.

This type of conversation has taken place many times in my life, as a youth worker and professor. The question I ask the students I mentor establishes a *covenant*—a mutual, agreed-upon, binding contract between two parties. The covenant is designed to emulate the godly arrangement that Jesus has with us.

Similarly, small church youth workers can use their friendships to touch their students' lives. Given their circumstances, a mentoring approach may be the most effective approach for many small churches. Keep in mind, not every youth worker has the ability to develop a model based on a mentoring approach. It's possible to combine it with other approaches or adapt it to available resources.

Mentoring roles within the church

- **The Discipler.** Discipling is the relational process in which a more experienced Christian shares with a newer one the commitment, understanding, and basic skills necessary for Christian growth.
- **The Spiritual Guide.** A spiritual guide is a mature Christian who shares her knowledge, skills, and basic philosophy about living a life devoted to God.
- **The Coach.** The coach provides a young Christian with motivation and teaches him the skills he needs to meet a task or challenge.
- **The Counselor.** A counselor offers timely advice from an unbiased

perspective on the other's self-image, relationships, circumstances, and ministry.
- **The Teacher.** A teacher imparts knowledge and understanding about a particular subject.
- **The Sponsor.** Sponsorship is a relational process in which a church member with credibility and authority works with a newer member to offer her the resources she'll need as a member of the church or part of a congregational group.
—from *Connecting: The Mentoring Relationships You Need to Succeed in Life*, Paul Stanley and J. Robert Clinton

> There is no substitute for genuine, authentic, real relationships within the Christian community. God uses people to grow and shape other people. We are God's gift to one another.

How do I use the mentoring approach to establish my program model?

A mentoring approach, like any other approach to developing a model for your youth ministry, must be individualized. But mentoring is impossible without authentic relationships. Steadfast commitment, demonstrated trust, and mutual love are the foundations of all meaningful relationships. Before real mentoring can begin, the exact nature of the relationship must be defined. A covenant must be formed.

> **In most cases, mentoring relationships are established by asking each other questions like these:**
> - *Are we determined to discover the calling and potential in each other?*
> - *Can we commit ourselves lovingly, sacrificially, and holistically to each other?*
> - *Are we willing to invest in and develop each other so that we become everything God wants us to be?*
>
> **The commitment to authentic relationships must be agreed upon before any real ministry can take place.**

Once a covenant has been made, there are a number of ways to begin mentoring. I've listed five principles for developing a model based on the mentoring approach:

1. Structure and Plan

Nothing truly significant happens in ministry without some kind of intention behind it. Therefore small church youth workers should develop a "vision statement." A vision statement should articulate the purpose of the mentoring program. In other words, clarify why it is necessary and what the goals for the participating students are.

It's also important to plan how mentoring will be implemented. Here are some questions that need to be answered in order to implement mentoring into your model.

- What students will benefit from participation?
- How will I invite students to participate?
- What available adults have the necessary qualifications to be mentors?
- How can I recruit these spiritually mature adults?
- How can I train these adults to be effective mentors?
- What materials can I use to train these adults?
- What times and places can these people meet?
- What resources and materials can I give to the adult mentors to aid them in the mentoring process?

2. Build Relationships

Everyone has core issues. Helping others get at them often makes the difference and a vital faith and a nonvital faith. If a youth worker can diagnose what core issues are gripping the lives of her students, figure out how to help them, and earn the right to help, she's in a position to make a huge impact on her students' lives. Adults who are good at this do the following:

- Use their intuition to sense what issues their students are concerned about.

- Ask specific, inviting, open-ended questions, and let students find their own answers.
- Respond to students quickly, offering helpful strategies and processes for change and growth. (This will be a *process;* there is no quick fix.)
- Communicate what it means to live in the "grace of God." (Students often assume God wants to punish them.)
- Reaffirm, periodically, their covenant to maintain honesty with each other.
- Pray regularly for wisdom from God. (A must!)
- Find students' greatest needs and develop strategies for meeting them. Then they'll see you and their faith as relevant.

3. Set Goals

For Christians, setting goals means recognizing ways in which we live our lives devoted to God. But mentoring means holding each other accountable to those goals, asking and answering honestly whether your lives reflect your devotion to God. While this process can be hard for junior highers, senior highers are more capable of this type of self-evaluation. The following tips can help you help your students achieve their goals:

- Demonstrate what it means to live a life devoted to God, not just what it means to practice devotion.
- Explain and live out the *immanence* of God (the immediate closeness and nearness, of God) when talking with your kids. Because students tend to view God as "way out there"—he's anything but!
- Have students and their mentors (this means you, too!) write their goals for areas of their lives they have trouble devoting to God. (Always ask the question, "What keeps me from devoting every area of my life to God?")

> Far too many times we only want to ask the hard, "juicy," embarrassing questions that, over a period of time, can serve as a source of discouragement. It's also important to ask what helped a student succeed and encourage him to keep doing that.

- Affirm your students by asking what helped them mature in specific areas of their lives.
- Teach them to practice the presence of God in their daily lives.

4. Develop Character

Kids need to know how to manage their lives. Youth workers can encourage students to use their gifts to benefit others as well as themselves. When kids realize they can make a difference in the lives of others by using their skills such as music, teaching, or athletics, they begin to overcome their own problems. When they develop self-worth, an ability to relate to the opposite sex, and anger management, for example, that's when their character develops.

In addition, adult leaders can help students develop healthy life-management skills. By tutoring with schoolwork, offering advice about work or family problems, or simply providing a safe place to ask for help, adults can help kids learn the skills they need to live well. Through these practical experiences, kids will hopefully develop positive characteristics they'll carry throughout their lives. Here's a list of character qualities that students can develop as they expand their life skills:

- **Faithfulness over success.** Being faithful to God is more important than looking good, making the most money, or having a lot of friends.
- **Excellence over being the best.** Striving for excellence in all you do is different from being the best.
- **Self-sacrifice over self-service.** Giving of yourself helps develop Christian maturity way, way more than serving yourself.
- **Authenticity over wearing masks.** What a person looks like inside is more important than what a person looks like on the outside.

> **Leadership is the faithful, passionate commitment to one's giftedness and calling.**

5. Develop Spiritual Leadership

When most students think of leadership, they imagine a person who can stand up in front of a bunch of people and get them to do something difficult. Not even close! Leadership roles and definitions are broad. And through mentoring, students can see the different forms of leadership modeled in relationships.

Every student, at least deep inside, wants to know that her life matters and that it has a purpose. Small church mentors can do a great service for their students, the church, and the world by helping their students discover their calling—and how they can use it to exercise leadership. Here are some areas in which students you're mentoring might be gifted:

- Music
- Teaching
- Acting
- Researching Scripture
- Lighting
- Cleaning
- Planning
- Mentoring younger kids

Of course, these are but a few of the almost infinite number of gifts your students might have. A mentor is in a unique position to help

> For we are God's workmanship, created in Christ Jesus to do good works, which God prepared in advance for us to do.
> —*Ephesians 2:10*

kids find their gifts. Because some kids get lost, even in small groups, the one-on-one mentoring relationship gives kids the chance to talk about what they love, not what the group enjoys or what others think it needs. This can help both mentors and students learn what type of leadership roles they might possess.

14

Alternative Approaches

What if my church doesn't fit into the contexts described and the approaches don't seem right?

Each church is different, and you must do what will work for your youth group. The situations and ideas I've offered should help the majority of small churches out there. But there are a number of small churches with even more specialized needs, concerns, and plans.

Although there are many others, two of the most prominent exceptions to the types of small churches I've discussed are the "not-yet-large" churches, urban churches, and churches with only one or two kids in the congregation. Some of what I've noted previously will apply to youth groups in these types of churches, but they also have some concerns that should be addressed separately.

What do I do if my small church and youth group are growing and we want to do a lot of outreach?

It's important to note that there's a type of small church that may not see discipleship as its primary calling. David Ray calls this the "not-yet-large church." Usually, this church is located in a high-growth area, is recently formed, or is denominationally independent with few established traditions. Sometimes it exists because of a church split. Because it's interested in growth and development, this type of church is more interested in outreach than in developing an inclusive congregation, discipleship, or mentoring.

This attitude means that, usually, not-yet-large churches are willing to give youth workers more resources, freedom, creativity, and flexibility in developing their programs. Often, they move faster when it comes to hiring a part- or full-time youth worker because the youth worker can reach many adolescents in the community. Also parents in the community can be reached if there's something to offer the kids.

What should I be concerned with if I work in a not-yet-large church?

Youth workers hired by not-yet-large churches should be aware that while they might have more flexibility than they would at other small churches, the pressure for them to produce is generally much greater. This is because most not-yet-large churches have tighter budgets than large churches—only with the same high expectations many large churches have. So, in essence, a youth worker may have to justify her existence more because the rest of the church expects her to alleviate the financial pressure on the church by bringing in more young parents with their children and teenagers.

In an effort to reclaim and revitalize a church that was virtually dead and had only a few members, Eric, the pastor, assessed the needs of the surrounding community. It was a high-growth area with a lot of young parents. He determined that a significant portion of the church's ministry would be to young parents and, eventually, parents with teenagers. There is little doubt that this was the reason Eric's church became one of the fastest-growing in the Pittsburgh diocese.

What if I'm in a small, inner-city church?

Another exception to the traditional small church is the small, urban church. This church has a number of problems that do not face any other church, large or small. While discipleship and mentoring are certainly important and possible in these churches, many would benefit simply from a "safe place" approach to youth ministry.

Mark Senter III describes a youth ministry model based on a safe-place approach. Here are some important characteristics of a safe-place youth group:

- Provides a safe environment so youth have somewhere other than the street to go. (Sometimes, even for rural kids, home isn't a safe place.)
- Provides facilities such as a gym, tutoring center, and room for Bible studies.
- Provides mentoring and guidance for troubled students.
- Provides, in some cases, essential needs (medical help, housing, legal advice, and counseling).
- Provides a place where social justice issues such as racism, poverty, employment, and drug addiction can be discussed openly and safely.

In order for small churches to take a safe-place approach to building a youth ministry model, a number of churches or community centers will have to pool their resources. In some cases, large, urban churches might be able to help, too.

What can I do if my church has only a few kids?

There are a number of churches that are so small they simply do not have enough kids for a regular youth ministry program. In some cases, there are only two or three teenagers in the congregation. What this means, though, is that the adults in these churches are in a great position to form lasting relationships with the kids. An inclusive congregational approach combined with a mentoring approach would probably be the most beneficial.

> Using the mentoring approach with the inclusive congregational approach can be a good way to get all church members involved in the lives of the youth. But this will only work if the entire church wants it.

However, there will be some hurdles. Churches with a small number of kids will need the commitment of adult members to make any sort of youth ministry work. Adults would have to be willing to spend time with teenagers and develop relationships with them. In addition, they'll need to be willing to deepen their own faith by asking and answering the same challenging questions anyone involved in discipleship or mentoring would ask.

> Not long ago, a colleague stopped me outside the building where we both teach. He asked whether I had a youth ministry student who might want to volunteer at his church. He had just been appointed to head a group to develop a youth ministry program. "The problem is," he said, "we only have four or five kids in our church." He wanted to know what he could do for such a small group. This is a perfect setting for a mentoring or inclusive congregational approach. Clearly, the church is concerned about its youth and wants to do something, but hiring someone or even asking an outsider to help is a bit too much for such a small group of kids. If the adults in their church become involved in their lives, the kids will feel important.

Five Types of Mentoring Relationships That Adults from Small Churches Can Initiate

1. *Traditional mentoring.* One adult and one teenager form a friendship, with the adult serving as a positive role model.
2. *Long-term, focused activity.* One adult is paired with one teenager to achieve a particular goal, usually academic (although not exclusively).
3. *Short-term, focused activity.* One adult is paired with one teenager to achieve a goal over a short period of time, such as a week or month. This is similar to the long-term focused activity, but it involves a shorter commitment.
4. *Team mentoring.* A family or team forms a friendship with one teenager who's often from a single-parent family.
5. *Group mentoring.* One adult volunteer builds a relationship with a small group (five or six) of young people.

—from research by Rebecca Saito and Dale Blyth,
Trend Watch

What if my church doesn't have the resources or number of interested adults to build any program for the youth?

Many small churches simply don't have the resources necessary to minister effectively to their kids. There's a great need among these churches to assess their situations accurately and determine if they can meet the spiritual (and mental and physical) needs of their youth. If they are really honest, they'll likely find they can't offer much because they simply lack the resources.

If they don't have the space, money, time, or interest from adults, these churches would benefit from cutting their youth programs loose. Too many times, the fear of losing kids to another church or even denomination keeps many small churches from encouraging their kids to participate in the youth group down the street.

Often networking with other churches (of same and different

denominations) in the community can give kids the Christian fellowship they need. Also, these churches might have better buildings or parents who can offer houses for events. If denominational differences are a problem, then establish a small group with the kids at your church to discuss these differences. If ego is a problem, get over it. The spiritual development of your students is more important than feeling

In one Presbyterian youth group, two or three kids from an Episcopalian church participated regularly. The Episcopalian church was small and didn't have anyone devoted specifically to youth ministry. Although the church leaders did involve the youth in the services and other aspects of the church, the kids needed to go somewhere that addressed their teenage needs. The Presbyterian church offered this. The youth pastor at the Presbyterian church talked and worked with the rector at the Episcopalian, and they planned a few events together.

like your church is better than the one down the street.

A number of small churches can create community by organizing a project that their limited groups rally around. This would work well for small churches that lack the traditional small-church attitudes. Choose a ministry that most of the youth care about and get involved! These ministries could range from working in the soup kitchen to tutoring younger children.

15

How Will You Spell Success?

How will I know if the youth ministry model I create is successful?

Successful youth ministry programs look different in each church. The best measure of success is your students. If they're growing into mature Christians who continue to develop their relationships with Jesus, you're probably doing what works.

If you feel you've done everything you can for the kids with what God has given you, you're probably doing what works.

It's important to remember, though, that the failure or success of a model or a program isn't important—the kids are. If you are serving them, you're definitely doing what works.

What I hope you've gotten from this book are some tools to help you serve your kids. This chapter reviews some of the main ideas and offers some of concluding thoughts.

> Because small churches are small for so many different reasons, small church youth workers must allow for flexibility in the youth ministry models they create. And if small church youth workers are aware of the limitations associated with youth ministry models, they can use them, or pieces of them, effectively to help provide a structure and overall sense of direction for their programs.

Most youth ministry models are adaptations of adaptations of something someone remembers someone else trying a long time ago. *Adapt, adapt, adapt.*

What are some ways I can test the effectiveness of my program?

By now, you should know that numbers are not the best way to measure your program's effectiveness. In fact, some of the biggest youth groups are the most ineffective at developing mature Christians. However, if you and your church are interested in growing, and outreach is one of your primary goals, then numbers might be a good way to determine if your program is effective. If there are a lot of kids at a particular church, then that church has a good outreach program.

Whatever your goals, there are a few questions that, if you answer them honestly, can help you determine if you're program is working.

- *Does my approach to creating a youth ministry program reflect my ministry context?* You must determine what goals you and your church have for the program. Your goals need to reflect the resources you have, the attitude of the congregation, and the kids' needs.

- *Am I using all my available resources?* Many small churches have marginal programs because they have not used all of their resources effectively. Make a list of all your resources and how they're being used.

- *Am I training the leaders, both adults and youth, so they have the resources necessary to lead their groups?* Although some people have a natural ability to lead groups and interact with others, they still need to be trained to handle difficult situations. They also need to continue to develop their own faith.

- *Can my students grow in their faith in a world that opposes it?* Students who leave youth groups for college or work often leave Christianity at the same time. One reason is the nature of the youth programs at their churches. These programs often teach "sin management"—how to avoid or control one's sin—rather than how to develop spiritual maturity and a desire to live for God. When confronted with the world, a kid needs a lot more than discipline and self-control—she needs God.

- *Do my students want to change the world for Christ? Do they have a relationship-with-God perspective or a heaven-versus-hell perspective?*

Resources come is a variety of shapes a sizes. Look for them in unexpected places. Here are some expected and unexpected ones:

- Church budget
- Volunteers
- Parents
- Building space
- Outdoor fields
- Books
- Church libraries
- Neighborhood churches
- Schools
- Community centers
- Kids' music equipment
- Parents' technical donations
- Parents' houses, pools, rec rooms, club memberships
- Congregational members
- Actors (kids and companies in the area)
- Group discounts at movie theaters and theme parks
- Community work projects
- Kids' artistic abilities
- Kids' athletic abilities
- Kids' older siblings who've gone to college or work
- Pastors
- National, state, and local parks

> **Approximately 75 percent of adolescents in church youth groups leave their Christian faith when they go to college.**
> **—George Barna**

Why shouldn't I leave spiritual development to the rest of the church and focus the youth program on outreach?

Focus on outreach isn't a bad thing, and if it's possible for your church, then it might be a really good thing! But spiritual development should be a part of *all* youth groups. If students aren't offered more than what they got initially, they'll stop coming. You might have five new students to replace that one who leaves, but that one could have reached 10 others if he had someone to help nurture his faith.

In *The Church Staff Handbook,* Harold J. Westing claims, "The process of our ministry is spiritual reproduction, not spiritual addition." He emphasizes the need to develop spiritually mature Christians rather than just converts. If our concern is merely to convert people to Christ, we may be selling short the world, the church, and ourselves.

Many well-intentioned small church youth workers, eager to make sure everybody knows about Christ, fail to do much with those students who already do. What they fail to understand is that if they had developed the small church's natural strength for discipleship, the strain produced from their concern about outreach could have been greatly reduced. Emphasizing discipleship as the primary approach to your program doesn't mean ignoring outreach and evangelism. In fact, over the long haul, it may actually enhance your outreach because you'll have more people who're able to reach out to others.

What should I remember as I begin to develop my own model of youth ministry?

Above all, you should take from this book whatever you need. But here are seven ideas that I think will help you the most:

1. Remember…different approaches to and models of youth ministry programs are helpful only in certain ministry contexts.

The following statistics from a report by George Barna reflect the lack of spiritual maturity in many teenagers who attend youth groups:

- Of those who call themselves Christians, 26 percent said they are "absolutely committed" and 57 percent said that they were "moderately committed" to the Christian faith.
- Almost two-thirds of teens (62 percent) believe the Bible is totally accurate in all of its teachings.
- 56 percent of born-again teens believe they have a personal responsibility to spread the Christian message.
- 29 percent of teens attend a weekly Bible study, prayer group, or Christian fellowship meeting, not including Sunday school or a 12-step program.

—BarnaResearch.com

2. Remember…approaches to and models of youth ministry programs can be blended to achieve a model that works best for each ministry context.

3. Remember…approaches to youth ministry depend on the *calling* and *personal gifts* of the youth worker as well as the needs of the church and kids.

4. Remember…the youth worker and her church must agree on the goals of the youth ministry program in order for it to work.

5. Remember…the youth worker must determine his ministry context before he can begin.

6. Remember…the youth worker must have a healthy ministry attitude about herself and the program.

7. Remember…ministry outcomes depend on the ministry contexts and ministry approaches.

8. Remember…small church youth ministry is just as important as youth ministry in any megachurch.

9. God bless you on your small church youth ministry journey!

Notes

Resources from Youth Specialties
www.youthspecialties.com

Ideas Library

Ideas Library on CD-ROM 2.0
Administration, Publicity, & Fundraising
Camps, Retreats, Missions, & Service Ideas
Creative Meetings, Bible Lessons, & Worship Ideas
Crowd Breakers & Mixers
Discussion & Lesson Starters
Discussion & Lesson Starters 2
Drama, Skits, & Sketches
Drama, Skits, & Sketches 2
Drama, Skits, & Sketches 3
Games
Games 2
Games 3
Holiday Ideas
Special Events

Bible Curricula

Backstage Pass to the Bible Kit
Creative Bible Lessons from the Old Testament
Creative Bible Lessons in 1 & 2 Corinthians
Creative Bible Lessons in Galatians and Philippians
Creative Bible Lessons in John
Creative Bible Lessons in Romans
Creative Bible Lessons on the Life of Christ
Creative Bible Lessons on the Prophets
Creative Bible Lessons in Psalms
Wild Truth Bible Lessons
Wild Truth Bible Lessons 2
Wild Truth Bible Lessons—Pictures of God
Wild Truth Bible Lessons—Pictures of God 2
Wild Truth Bible Lessons—Dares from Jesus

Topical Curricula

Creative Junior High Programs from A to Z, Vol. 1 (A-M)
Creative Junior High Programs from A to Z, Vol. 2 (N-Z)
Girls: 10 Gutsy, God-Centered Sessions on Issues That Matter to Girls
Guys: 10 Fearless, Faith-Focused Sessions on Issues That Matter to Guys
Good Sex
The Justice Mission
Live the Life! Student Evangelism Training Kit
The Next Level Youth Leader's Kit
Roaring Lambs
So What Am I Gonna Do with My Life?
Student Leadership Training Manual
Student Underground
Talking the Walk
What Would Jesus Do? Youth Leader's Kit
Wild Truth Bible Lessons
Wild Truth Bible Lessons 2
Wild Truth Bible Lessons—Pictures of God
Wild Truth Bible Lessons—Pictures of God 2
Wild Truth Bible Lessons—Dares from Jesus

Discussion Starters

Discussion & Lesson Starters (Ideas Library)
Discussion & Lesson Starters 2 (Ideas Library)
EdgeTV
Every Picture Tells a Story
Get 'Em Talking
Keep 'Em Talking!
Good Sex Drama
Have You Ever...?
Name Your Favorite
Unfinished Sentences
What If...?
Would You Rather...?
High School TalkSheets—Updated!
More High School TalkSheets—Updated!
High School TalkSheets from Psalms and Proverbs—Updated!
Junior High-Middle School TalkSheets—Updated!
More Junior High-Middle School TalkSheets—Updated!
Junior High-Middle School TalkSheets from Psalms and Proverbs—Updated!
Real Kids Ultimate Discussion-Starting Videos:
Castaways
Growing Up Fast
Hardship & Healing
Quick Takes
Survivor
Word on the Street
Small Group Qs

Drama Resources

Drama, Skits, & Sketches (Ideas Library)
Drama, Skits, & Sketches 2 (Ideas Library)
Drama, Skits, & Sketches 3 (Ideas Library)
Dramatic Pauses
Good Sex Drama
Spontaneous Melodramas
Spontaneous Melodramas 2
Super Sketches for Youth Ministry

Game Resources

Games (Ideas Library)
Games 2 (Ideas Library)
Games 3 (Ideas Library)
Junior High Game Nights
More Junior High Game Nights
Play It!
Screen Play CD-ROM

Additional Programming Resources
(also see Discussion Starters)

The Book of Uncommon Prayer
Camps, Retreats, Missions, & Service Ideas (Ideas Library)
Creative Meetings, Bible Lessons, & Worship Ideas (Ideas Library)

Crowd Breakers & Mixers (Ideas Library)
Everyday Object Lessons
Great Fundraising Ideas for Youth Groups
More Great Fundraising Ideas for Youth Groups
Great Retreats for Youth Groups
Great Talk Outlines for Youth Ministry
Holiday Ideas (Ideas Library)
Incredible Questionnaires for Youth Ministry
Kickstarters
Memory Makers
Special Events (Ideas Library)
Videos That Teach
Videos That Teach 2
Worship Services for Youth Groups

Quick Question Books

Have You Ever...?
Name Your Favorite
Unfinished Sentences
What If...?
Would You Rather...?

Videos & Video Curricula

Dynamic Communicators Workshop
EdgeTV
The Justice Mission
Live the Life! Student Evangelism Training Kit
Make 'Em Laugh!
Purpose-Driven® Youth Ministry Training Kit
Real Kids Ultimate Discussion-Starting Videos:
        Castaways
        Growing Up Fast
        Hardship & Healing
        Quick Takes
        Survivors
        Word on the Street
Student Underground
Understanding Your Teenager Video Curriculum
Youth Ministry Outside the Lines

Especially for Junior High

Creative Junior High Programs from A to Z, Vol. 1 (A-M)
Creative Junior High Programs from A to Z, Vol. 2 (N-Z)
Junior High Game Nights
More Junior High Game Nights
Junior High-Middle School TalkSheets—Updated!
More Junior High-Middle School TalkSheets—Updated!
Junior High-Middle School TalkSheets from Psalms and Proverbs—Updated!
Wild Truth Journal for Junior Highers
Wild Truth Bible Lessons
Wild Truth Bible Lessons 2
Wild Truth Journal—Pictures of God
Wild Truth Bible Lessons—Pictures of God
Wild Truth Bible Lessons—Dares from Jesus
Wild Truth Journal—Dares from Jesus

Student Resources

Backstage Pass to the Bible: An All-Access Tour of the New Testament
Backstage Pass to the Bible: An All-Access Tour of the Old Testament
Grow for It! Journal through the Scriptures
So What Am I Gonna Do with My Life?
Spiritual Challenge Journal: The Next Level
Teen Devotional Bible
What (Almost) Nobody Will Tell You about Sex
What Would Jesus Do? Spiritual Challenge Journal

Clip Art

Youth Group Activities (print)
Clip Art Library Version 2.0 (CD-ROM)

Digital Resources

Clip Art Library Version 2.0 (CD-ROM)
Great Talk Outlines for Youth Ministry
Hot Illustrations CD-ROM
Ideas Library on CD-ROM 2.0
Screen Play
Youth Ministry Management Tools

Professional Resources

Administration, Publicity, & Fundraising (Ideas Library)
Dynamic Communicators Workshop
Great Talk Outlines for Youth Ministry
Help! I'm a Junior High Youth Worker!
Help! I'm a Small Church Youth Worker!
Help! I'm a Small-Group Leader!
Help! I'm a Sunday School Teacher!
Help! I'm an Urban Youth Worker!
Help! I'm a Volunteer Youth Worker!
Hot Illustrations for Youth Talks
More Hot Illustrations for Youth Talks
Still More Hot Illustrations for Youth Talks
Hot Illustrations for Youth Talks 4
How to Expand Your Youth Ministry
How to Speak to Youth...and Keep Them Awake at the Same Time
Junior High Ministry (Updated & Expanded)
Just Shoot Me
Make 'Em Laugh!
The Ministry of Nurture
Postmodern Youth Ministry
Purpose-Driven® Youth Ministry
Purpose-Driven® Youth Ministry Training Kit
So That's Why I Keep Doing This!
Teaching the Bible Creatively
Your First Two Years in Youth Ministry
A Youth Ministry Crash Course
Youth Ministry Management Tools
The Youth Worker's Handbook to Family Ministry